Group of International Communists

FUNDAMENTAL PRINCIPLES OF COMMUNIST PRODUCTION AND DISTRIBUTION

Group of International Communists
FUNDAMENTAL PRINCIPLES OF
COMMUNIST PRODUCTION AND
DISTRIBUTION
© 2020 Hermann Lueer (Editor/Translator)
herluee@yahoo.com
Red & Black Books
Bordesholmer Straße 22
22143 Hamburg, Germany
All rights reserved
Cover: Niki Bong
mail@bongolai.de
ISBN:9798615430794

Objective

The development of capitalism is leading to increasingly serious crises, reflected in ever-increasing unemployment and an ever-deeper disruption of the production system, leaving millions of workers out of production and starving to death. At the same time, the contradictions between the different nations are increasing, as a result of which the economic war leads to a new world war.

Increasing impoverishment and growing insecurity of existence force the working class to begin the struggle for the communist mode of production. In this struggle, the Group of International Communists encourages the workers to take over the management and administration of production and distribution **themselves** in accordance with generally adopted social rules to realize the **Association of Free and Equal Producers**.

The GIC sees the essential progress of the workers' movement in the development of workers' self-confidence. Therefore, it confronts the leading politics of the parliamentary parties and the trade union movement with the slogan:

<u>**All power to the workers' councils**</u>

Production in the hands of the enterprise organizations

GIC

- FOREWORD BY THE EDITOR — 8
- FOREWORD TO THE FIRST EDITION — 12
- FOREWORD TO THE SECOND EDITION — 13

1. THE STARTING POINTS OF THE FUNDAMENTAL PRINCIPLES OF COMMUNIST PRODUCTION AND DISTRIBUTION — 17

2. THE SOCIAL DEMOCRATIC "REVISION" OF MARXISM — 27

3. THE UNIT OF ACCOUNT IN COMMUNISM — 55

4. PROGRESS IN THE FORMULATION OF THE PROBLEM — 67

5. LIBERTARIAN COMMUNISM — 84

6. THE SOCIAL PRODUCTION PROCESS IN GENERAL — 101

7. THE COMMUNIST PRODUCTION — 104

8. THE SOCIALLY AVERAGE WORKING HOUR AS THE BASIS OF PRODUCTION! — 123

9.
THE SOCIAL AVERAGE WORKING HOUR AS THE BASIS FOR CONSUMPTION _____ 139

10.
THE GENERAL SOCIAL WORK _____ 159

11.
THE ACCOUNTING AS AN IDEATIONAL SUMMARY OF THE PRODUCTION AND DISTRIBUTION PROCESS _____ 184

12.
THE ABOLITION OF THE MARKET _____ 193

13.
THE EXPANSION OF PRODUCTION _____ 214

14.
THE CONTROL OF THE OPERATING LIFE _____ 228

15.
THE INTRODUCTION OF COMMUNISM IN AGRICULTURE _____ 257

16.
THE ECONOMIC DICTATORSHIP OF THE PROLETARIAT _____ 273

17.
FINAL CONSIDERATIONS _____ 277

APPENDIX _____ 290

LITERATURE _____ 301

Foreword by the editor

Karl Marx's critique of capitalism has received worldwide attention - from those who want to overcome capitalism, but also from bourgeois intellectuals who don't like the critique of capitalism.

Understandably, the bourgeois intellectuals are not interested in the alternative to capitalism. But how can it be explained that the alternative to capitalism, which can be derived from Marx's critique of capitalism, has not received any attention from the critics of capitalism? Why is the *"Association of Free and Equal People"* that Marx and Engels sketched out in their critique of capitalism taken seriously, if at all, only as an idealistic picture of the future? Although Marx and Engels, with their reference to the calculation of working hours as the foundation for the relationship between producer and product, have themselves named the *economic basis* for the new production relationship and thus for the independent, direct construction of the "Association of Free and Equal People". So, how can it be explained that the first scientific elaboration of what Marx and Engels only hinted at in their critique of capitalism met with no interest among critics of capitalism?

The explanation is very simple. The intellectuals critical of capitalism do not like the alternative that has been presented.

For the communist parties fighting for the leading power, the idea is perfectly natural that the workers in the factories take over the power to hand it over to the intellectual vanguard so that the latter can then organize the new society in the "name and for the good of the working class". The idea that the workers in the factories take over power in order to control their relationship from producer to product *themselves* based on the calculation of working hours, without the need for privileged leadership, does not fit in with their idea of a centrally structured economic and administrative apparatus.

But also the "libertarian communists" do not like the *economic basis* of the "Association of Free and Equal People", as shown by Marx and Engels. They want to live in a communist society and, at the same time, be free from it. They dream of an immediate transition to a self-determined society of free and equal people according to the motto "from each according to his abilities, to each according to his needs", for which every binding economic basis seems to them a contradiction.

The "party communists" rely on the dictatorship over the proletariat, on whose distant horizon freedom appears after the "realm of necessity" has been overcome under the leadership of the party through the long and complicated path of the development of the productive forces. The "libertarian communists" rely on the socialist morality freely hovering above the economy in order to establish the "realm of freedom" in the "realm of necessity" without the measure of the calculation of working hours, which according to Marx, is the *unavoidable* measure. While the attempts of state communism with the dictatorship over the proletariat ended in a return to capitalism, in 1936 in Spain, the attempts of libertarian communists ended in economic chaos, in which the libertarian communists themselves sought their salvation in forms of central allocation.

The "Fundamental Principles of Communist Production and Distribution" are *"the last message that the revolutionary movements of the 1st half of the 20th century have left us."* [1] They show the economic basis on which exploitation can be abolished and communist society realized without sinking into chaos and without reducing communist society to an ideal on the distant horizon of human history. In this sense, the German translation of the second completely revised and expanded edition of the "Fundamental Principles" is at the same time a fundamental cri-

---

[1] Henk Canne Meijer, Die Arbeiterrätebewegung in Deutschland (1918 - 1933) (The Origins of the Movement for Workers' Councils in Germany), Edition Soziale Revolution 1985)

tique of the various theories and also of the practices of the various currents that refer to Marxism, anarchism or, more generally, socialism. A critique that has lost none of its original topicality to this day. Or, in the words of the GIC:

"There is no point in discussing "federalism or centralism" if you don't first show what the economic basis of this "federalism" or this "centralism" will be. In reality, the forms of organization of a given economy are not, on the whole, arbitrary forms, they are derived from the principles of that economy itself. ... Therefore it is insufficient to present the economy of communism only as a negation of the capitalist system: no money, no market, no private or state property. It is necessary to present its positive characters, to show what the economic laws will be, that will triumph over those of capitalism. If one proceeds in this way, it is very likely that the alternative "federalism or centralism" appears to be the wrong question." [2]

February 2020, Hermann Lueer

---

[2] Henk Canne Meijer, Die Arbeiterrätebewegung in Deutschland (1918 - 1933) (The Origins of the Movement for Workers' Councils in Germany), Edition Soziale Revolution 1985

Foreword to the first edition

These "Fundamental Principles" were developed over four years of discussion within the group of International Communists. The first edition was published in German in 1930 in the publishing house of the revolutionary company organizations organized in the Allgemeinen Arbeiter Union Deutschlands (AAUD) - "Neue Arbeiterverlag," Berlin.

Due to financial difficulties, we couldn't publish a Dutch edition in ordinary book form. Therefore, we used a less widespread publication method, the partial publication as an appendix to the Persmateriaal van de Internationale Communisten (P.I.C.). We have made a virtue of necessity by looking through the entire manuscript so that this edition is not identical with the German one. No substantial changes have been made to the content, but the structure and various formulations have been changed and, we believe, improved.

We hope that these fundamental principles will lead to a detailed discussion and contribute to more clarity and unity about the goal of the revolutionary proletariat, so that the forces, which are still differently oriented, will unite in a unified current.

June 1931, GIC

Foreword to the second edition

The discussion about the first edition of these "Fundamental Principles" has shown that this book is often seen as a kind of "plan," which must be propagated diligently until the masses have become familiar with the economic organization based on working hours.

This, of course, can never be the intention of the authors, who are based on historical materialism. The entirety of the views that we can summarize in one word as the "ideal of the future" does not arise "through the books" or oral propaganda. These do not have much more than an ordering function. They can only make conscious the truth of experience and bring it into a more general context. The masses hardly read or do not read at all, but from the practice of everyday life, certain views are evoked as political and economic ideal. At present, the political-economic ideal of the masses, both socialist and communist and Catholic, Christian, and neutral workers, is that the state should be the great general representative of their interests. The practical effect of this is that the masses are focused on state capitalism, even if they are not aware of it.

This state-capitalist orientation of the masses did not come about through propaganda or "through the books," but crystallized as the experiential truth of the time that lies behind us. In the previous era of parliamentary struggles for social reforms, the development of trade unions, in which unions became semi-state corporations, the masses experienced an increase in their standard of living compared to, for example, 100 years earlier. This, in their view, made the state the great lever that would increasingly order social life for their salvation, and led to the idea that the repressive state of the past should become the general "welfare state." That is why National Socialism could and can anchor itself so deeply in the broad masses.

In the coming period of the class struggle, the fighting conditions are completely different. The parliamentary democracy of the political parties and the economic democracy of the collective agreements no longer work to the advantage of the masses, so that they are voluntarily or reluctantly driven into mass actions under their own leadership. Besides, the state no longer appears to be an improver of living standards, but a direct representative of big business. In this massive struggle between capital and labor, which includes an entire development period, the ideal of the future of state capitalism rotates with the notions of class struggle. Every mass action under their own leadership shows in small detail what will one day be the general principle of social life: Here the masses take their destiny into their own hands by carrying out all the tasks necessary for the struggle either themselves or through functionaries chosen by them and subordinated to them. The coming process of development is an ascent to this growth of the class unit. And only when this class unit has become the common property of the masses does it have the power to overthrow capitalism. And only in this sense can it be said that the new society is born out of the womb of the old. The self-determination of the masses, born from the necessity of struggle, then becomes the guiding principle of the new organization of social life. There, the class struggle itself is the actual driving force in the destruction of the state-capitalist future ideal of the masses.

So, this book can never replace this class struggle. It only wants to express economically what will happen politically. For this, it was necessary not to take the abolition of private property in means of production as a starting point, but the abolition of wage labor.

All thoughts based on this. And our research leads us to the conclusion that the workers who came to power in mass movements can only hold this political power if they abolish wage labor in economic life by taking working time as the central axis around which economic life moves.

Finally, a few remarks. The German edition of this work, which was put on the market by the General Workers Union in 1930, was confiscated and destroyed. A summary of the book published in German in *Kampfsignal* - New York and in English in *Council Correspondence* - Chicago. With the reorientation of the revolutionary groups within the German working class, we find a group that, for the first time in the German worker's movement, combines the struggle for the worker's councils directly with the introduction of communism based on working hours. Work here is the central category that regulates the mutual relations of people in social life; it is the basis for the new legal relations.

No fundamental changes have been made to this second edition compared with the first. Some chapters have been slightly expanded. For example, "State Communism and Wage Labor", paying particular attention to the fact that the same right to consumer goods is practically an unequal right. A new chapter on production control has been added.

January 1935, GIC

1.
The starting points of the Fundamental Principles of Communist Production and Distribution

a. The workers' councils as the organizational basis

In our paper "The Fundamental Principles of Communist Production and Distribution", the implementation of communism is seen from a completely different side than has been customary in the labor movement until now. In part, the course of the Russian revolution is the cause, which put the need for a closer examination of the problems of communist economic life on the agenda.

A further reason for the need for further investigation is the new position of agricultural problems. In our paper – "Lines of development in agriculture" – we have shown that agricultural production is completely socialized. That the farm has changed over to "industrial production", but that nevertheless, the agricultural question remains the big obstacle, making it impossible to carry out the "socialism" or "communism" of the common view. The farm cannot be integrated organically into the "communist economy". We conclude from this that then the entire understanding of this communism must be wrong.

The third, and probably the most important reason why an examination of the problems of communist production became necessary, was that the working class used different forms of organization **in the revolution** than in the period of quiet "improvement of working conditions". The organizational structure of the revolutionary workers' movement finds its manifestation in the **factory organizations and workers' councils**.

Between the organizational structure of a movement and the ideologies, the world of thought, through which it is carried, however, is a close association. This connection is so intimate that the structure can be called a function of its ideologies. The organizational structure of the various currents in the workers' movement then runs parallel to the various views we encounter on the construction of communist society. If we also see structural changes in the class struggle, then this indicates that important ideological transformations have taken place, which are now finding their organizational expression.

In revolutionary periods, important ideological transformations take place at unprecedented speed.

The goal of the workers becomes completely different, completely radicalized. One of the most important lessons that the revolutionary period of 1917-23 brought us is probably that the transformed ideologies have a different organizational expression than the old workers' movement. Most violently, even in a bloody struggle, the old workers' movement is opposed because it opposes the newly formed world of thought of the radicalized workers. The *factory organizations* and *worker's councils* are the organizational weapons with which the workers carry out the revolution.

The importance attached to the idea of councils at the beginning of the revolutionary period can be seen, for example, from an overview by D.J. Struik in "De Nieuwe Tijd" (Vol. 1919, p. 466) from the resolution on the councils adopted by the K.P.H. at that time.

It says there:

»Nothing shows more clearly the progress we have made in recognizing the laws of the social revolution than our explanation of the council system. Even two years ago, that declaration was still utterly impossible, and three years ago, even the brightest minds of the International could say almost nothing about the significance of the councils as we see them now. It will be difficult to find expressions in this spirit in pre-war literature ... Everywhere until the February Revolution of

1917, it remains a simple announcement of the necessary change ... in the political and economic forms in which the revolution was to be wrapped. As far as we know, no further indications of this have been made, at least not on this side of the Vistula. Rosa Luxemburg writes casually only once in her entire brochure on the mass strike about the 1905 Council of Workers' Delegates. Trotsky deals in detail with the history, significance, and power of this first council in his book on the first Russian revolution. Still, he does not delve into an investigation of the council system itself. And even in the Marxist writings that appeared during the first half of the world war, in "Vorboten", "Lichtstrahlen", etc., there is no reference to the Petrograd Soviet of 1905. The fact that shortly after the outbreak of the February Revolution of 1917, the Soviet idea began to have such a firm foundation is exclusively a consequence of the practice of the revolution ... If ever Mehring's word that the "intuition of the acting masses can be more ingenious than the greatest genius," is true, it is in this case.«

The most important, most positive thing that the revolutionary period of 1917-23 has brought us is that we have seen the forms in which the proletarian revolution takes place, while at the same time, the ideologies appeared, the expression of which are the new forms. The takeover of the social productive apparatus is carried out by the factory organizations and their unification, the workers' councils. Therefore, an examination of the problems of communist production and distribution must start from this basis.³

b. The Marxist explanation of the domination of the working class

In addition to the factory organization, the second starting point for the fundamental principles of communist economic life is the Marxist explanation of the **domination** and **exploitation** of the working class in capitalist society. It is not primarily an interpretation of "Marx quotations", but rather the general train of thought, the essence of his analysis.

Domination and exploitation are extraordinarily simple in their causes and immediately comprehensible for everyone: they are enclosed in the fact that the worker is separated from the means of production. The capitalist is the owner of the means of production - the worker owns only his labor power; - the capitalist owns the conditions under which the worker must work. Thus, the worker is *economically* completely without rights (even if political democracy is carried out to the extreme), he is dependent on capital. With the **right of disposal** over the means of production, the possessing class also has

---

³ The poem "De Arbeidersraad" by Herman Gorter, which concludes this section in the Dutch version, has been omitted here because it cannot be adequately translated in its poem form.

the disposal over the labor power; that is, **it rules the working class**.

The right of disposal over the means of production, exercised by the ruling class, brings the working class into a relationship of dependence on capital.

That is the essence!

The fact that the working class is separated from the means of production implies that it does not dispose of the finished product. The workers have nothing to do with the goods produced by them; they do not belong to them, but their "employers". What further happens with them is not their business; they only have to sell their labor power and receive their "wage" in return: they are **wage laborers**.

That cannot be otherwise. The disposition of the production apparatus includes the disposition of the finished product. They are two different sides of the same thing. They are functionally dependent, and one is not without the other; one exists only *through* the other. *Because* the workers do not have the disposal of the production apparatus, *therefore* they also do not have the disposal of the finished product; *thereby* they are dominated, *thereby* they are wage laborers.

Wage labor is the expression of the fact that the work is separated from the work products, the fact that the workers have no say about the product, nor about the production apparatus. *Wage labor* is the unmistakable sign of the "immaturity" of the working class, of its domination by those who dispose of the social production apparatus and the social product.

As simple as the basis for the domination of the working class is, as simple is the *formulation* for the abolition of wage slavery (even if the practical implementation is not so simple!). This abolition can only consist in the abolition of the separation of work and the work product, that the *right of disposal* over the work product and therefore also over the means of production is again given to the workers.

That is the essence of communist production.

Of course, this can no longer be done in the way that the craftsman used to have his tools and work product at his disposal. Today's society does not know anymore "individual" work on its own; it has gone over to social production, to the socialized work process, where everyone is only a cog in the big whole. That is why the workers must now possess the means of production *collectively*. But common possession, which does not at the same time include the right of disposal over it, misses its purpose.

Common ownership is not an **end in itself**. It is only the **means** to make possible the right of disposal over the means of production for the workers, to abolish the separation of work and product of labor, to abolish wage labor.

c. The confusion of goal and means

This is the weak point of today's labor movement. The aim is to bring the means of production into common ownership, and they do not suspect that this cannot be the **goal** at all; they do not suspect that the transition to "common ownership" only poses the problem of a new mode of production. The working class wrongly lives in the confidence that communism must come "by itself" when private ownership of means of production is abolished. But the assumption that in doing so, wage labor must necessarily disappear, is wrong.

The *real proletarian goal* can only be for the workers to conquer the right of disposal over the means of production (and thus over the product), and thereby indeed, abolish wage labor. Only then will the working class become "free". The common disposition of production by *free producers* is the basis of communist society.

The free producers, however, cannot *arbitrarily* dispose of the means of production, as the "free producers" in capitalism (the factory owners or "leaders") do. If the disposal is arbitrary, then there can be no question of *common disposal*. The first condition to make common disposal of the production apparatus possible is therefore that the production takes place according to generally established rules, rules on which *all* social work must rest. Only then can joint decision-making and action be achieved. The independent producers must, therefore, create *equal production rules* for all producers. Thus, the free producers at the same time become *equal producers*. The operational organizations thus embody, in their connections of the most varied kind: **"The Association of Free and Equal Producers"**.

Seen from this point of view, therefore, the demand for "equality" does not appear to be an "ethical" or "moral" one at all, but rather arises from the necessary production conditions of communist economic life. Here, "equality" is not an ethical term, but an economic one: it wants to express nothing other than that production in all business organizations proceeds according to the same rules in order to make possible a common disposition of the production apparatus. To make these rules binding for the whole production is the essential task of a proletarian revolution.

So, we see how the moral demand of equality that we put on communism, the demand of the same conditions for the development of individuality, finds its foundation in the equality in production.

2.
The social democratic "revision" of Marxism

a. The social work and the organizational forms in which the capital dominates this work are confused.

The radical social democracy (Bolsheviks) and the reformist have both revised the Marxist doctrine precisely in the decisive point of the "association of free and equal producers". In the Marxist sense, the socialization of the working process is nothing other than the fact that the "production of commodities" becomes the dominant mode of production in the course of development. More and more circles of producers work exclusively for the market. Everyone produces what he does not consume himself, and the manufactured product is for others; - everyone thereby does social work, everyone works for society. Capitalism itself is the great revolutionary who, in the course of development, tore producers away from their old mode of production and threw them into the service of capital in a working process that abolished the old patriarchal working conditions that broke every relationship with the person or family. Capitalism brought everyone into a state that everyone, stripped of all possessions, has nothing but his naked labor power to participate in the socialized labor process.

Social democracy did (and does) something completely different about the process of the socialization of production. It saw the constant progress of social production in the continuous growth of trust, syndicate, and cartel formation. It saw socialization in the form in which the social mode of production *organizes itself*. In reality, this is nothing other than the form in which the private-capitalist (or collective-capitalist) *right of disposal* over the means of production, over social work and over the social product *is organized and concentrated*. Social democracy confuses the specific capitalist forms of organization of the *domination* of social work with social work itself!

This confusion also occurs among the Bolsheviks, who see communism as a "national economy" modeled on modern state-owned enterprises such as railways and postal services.

It is no wonder that in this confusion of concepts, the view of socialism also takes a completely different direction from the Marxist view of social work. Both for radical social democracy and reformist democracy, the *vertical trust* - the capitalist form of the organization of the production process from the raw material to the finished product - thus becomes the ideal state of the communist mode of production. »*To organize the whole economy on the lines of the postal service ... that is our immediate aim.*«[4]

It is obvious that the way to socialism is thus portrayed to the working class in the sense that it conquers political power, seizes the state, and at the same time has the central apparatus of production, created by capital itself, in its hands.

Thus, the well-known left-wing Marxist "Parvus" shows

»*how easy the transition from large-scale industry to state production can be.*«[5]

The same goes for Rudolf Hilferding:

»*That means nothing other than that our generation is faced with the problem of transforming, with the help of the state, with the help of conscious social regulation, this economy organized and led by the capitalists into an economy led by the democratic state.*«[6]

---

[4] W. I. Lenin, State and Revolution, Works Vol. 25, p. 432
[5] A, Parvus, Der Staat, die Industrie und der Sozialismus 1919 (The State, Industry and Socialism), p. 112
[6] Rudolf Hilferding, Die Aufgaben der Sozialdemokratie in der Republik, p. 6., Speech at the party conference in Kiel, May 1927

This is the general view of communist production that we find in all shades within social democracy. The differences only occur when it comes to the means, to the tactics with which one wants to achieve this social state.

The reformist social democracy wants it through universal suffrage, exploiting bourgeois democracy. It wants to "conquer" **this** bourgeois-capitalist state, and through it, subjugate the organizations of capital. However, the reality is that the state, with the social democrats in government, is subdued by the organization of capital.

The radical Social Democracy (Bolsheviks) is resolutely fighting this policy. It propagates the annihilation of the bourgeois state in revolution and the formation of new political power by the political organization of the working class – the state of the proletarian dictatorship. Through this state, a central economic organization is to be created by revolutionary means - after the model of the capitalist trust (Lenin) - in which the enterprises and industries are taken up as far as they are "ripe" for it. In other words, the branches of industry that are sufficiently concentrated by capital to be accepted into state administration are to be *"nationalized"*.

b. "Nationalizing" and "Socializing"

Although Marx did not give a "description" of communist economic life, there can be no doubt that, in his opinion, the regulation of production should come about

»not by the state, but through the connection of the free associations of a socialist society.«[7]

A view which, according to reformist Cunow, Marx adopted from the liberal-anarchist movements of his time. Management and administration of production should fall directly to the *producers and consumers themselves* and not on the detour via the state. The equality of state and society is only an invention of the later years.

In the years 1880-90, this point of view was still shared by social democracy. So said, e.g., the old Liebknecht in a speech on the occasion of the attempts to bring the railways, coal mines and other large industries into state administration: *»The more bourgeois society realizes that in the long run, it cannot defend itself against the onslaught of socialist ideas, the closer we are to the moment when state socialism will be proclaimed in full earnestness, and the last struggle that social democracy will*

---

[7] H. Cunow: "The Marxian History, Social and State Theory", 1, p. 309

have to fight will be fought out under the battle cry: "Here social democracy-- There state socialism".«

Cunow remarks: *»Accordingly, the party congress declared itself against nationalization; for social democracy and state socialism are "irreconcilable opposites«.*[8]

This position was abandoned at the turn of the century, while the nationalization or communal management of enterprises was presented as a gradual advancement towards socialism. In social democratic terminology, such enterprises are also called "public enterprises", although the producers have nothing to do with their administration and management.

The Russian Revolution also took place in the spirit of the "nationalization" of industry. Here, too, the "ripe" branches of industry were incorporated into the central state apparatus. In 1917 the producers began to expropriate the owners of various companies, much to the discomfort of those who wanted to manage and administer economic life "from above". The workers wanted to organize production on new bases according to communist rules.

---

[8] H. Cunow: "The Marxian History, Social and State Theory", 1, p. 340

Instead of these rules, they were fobbed off with empty words: The Communist Party issued guidelines according to which companies had to form trusts in order to bring them under central administration. What could not be included in the central right of disposal was returned to the owners because these companies were not yet "ripe". The first All-Russian Congress of Economic Councils passed the following resolution accordingly:

»In the field of production organization, a final nationalization is necessary. It is necessary to move from the nationalization of individual enterprises (so far 304) to the consequential nationalization of the industry. Nationalization may not be an "occasional" nationalization. It may only be carried out by the Supreme Economic Council or the Council of People's Representatives with the approval of the Supreme Economic Council.«

So, the Communist Party did not give guidelines according to which the workers *themselves* could integrate their enterprise into the communist economic life, and it did not give guidelines according to which management and administration actually passed to society. For them, the liberation of the

---

[9] A. Goldschmidt, Die Wirtschaftsorganisation Sowjet-Russlands (Economic Organization in Soviet Russia), p. 42. Highlighting by GIC

workers was not the work of the workers themselves, but the implementation of communism was a function of the "men of science," the "intellectuals," the "statisticians," and so on. The Communist Party believed it only needed to chase away the old industrial leaders and take command of the work itself to direct everything to the safe haven of communism. The working class was just good enough to sweep away the old rulers of labor – and put new ones in their place. Their function did not go further, and it could not go further either, because generally established rules of production did not provide the basis for self-organization.

The Bolsheviks, who are forcefully proclaiming to the world that they are consistent followers of Marx, would do well to be a little less noisy. They are consistent in revising Marx, because the transformation of the *socialization of production* as Marx saw it, into the "nationalization" of the "ripe" enterprises, is nothing other than the abandonment of the proletarian revolution, the abandonment of communism itself. In the Marxist sense, there are no "ripe" or "not ripe" enterprises, but society **as a whole** is ripe for communism. Very rightly noted F. Oppenheimer in the anthology by H. Beck on "Wege und Ziel der Sozialisierung" on page 16/17:

»They believe that they are gradually approaching Marxist socialization by calling the nationalization or municipalization of individual enterprises socialization. Hence the otherwise incomprehensible mysterious turn of the "ripe" enterprises. From Marx's point of view, this is ... pure nonsense. For him, a socialist society can only be "ripe" as a whole. Individual enterprises or branches of enterprises can be just as little ripe and "socialized" in this sense as the individual organs of an embryo are ripe in the fourth month of pregnancy and can be delivered separately to independent existence.«

c. The Right of Command over the Working Class in State Communism

What in social democracy of all shades is considered socialism or communism is nothing more than a consistent introduction of the forms of organization that capital adopts in and through its process of concentration. But what does the organization of production created by capital mean? What does it mean on the one hand from the point of view of the wage workers and on the other hand from the point of view of the capitalists?

It is the domination of labor, the organized domination of wage laborers!

The Marxist analysis of capitalism leaves no doubt about it. Marx has characterized the social position of the capitalist vis-à-vis the wage-worker as having the disposal over the work, i.e., over the workers in production.

The socialization theories of all directions of social democracy all revolve around this one point of domination of the working class. That labor must be controlled and commanded is self-evident for them, and that for this (because it is about a socially unbreakably connected system), a tight central organization is necessary, is just as "natural". The task one sets oneself is to organize the command over the workers as comprehensively and centrally as possible but to place this command itself under the control of the parliament (with the reformists) or the proletarian state formed by the political party of the wage workers (Bolsheviks). In other words, the domination of the working class is to be tempered by "democracy".

Within this framework, the directions of the so-called "Marxist" workers' movement are moving, from the genuine reformists to the outspoken revolutionaries who want to destroy today's economic and political organization of society in order to re-organize it.

The result is always an apparatus of power with the authority of command over the wage laborers.

If the socialist production system is to function after these socialization projects, then the management must above all be concerned with securing the disposal of the production apparatus and thus the right of command over the workers. In theory, this is demanded in order to defend itself against counterrevolution; in practice, it is also directed against any undesirable interference on the part of the wage workers. If the workers themselves want to determine the course of production, this striving is presented as an outflow of bourgeois thinking, and – these workers are treated as counterrevolutionaries.

The development of Russian state communism is an instructive example of this!

What is to be achieved now with the central management of economic life established by the parliament or the political party of wage workers? Everyone agrees that exploitation should be abolished. The reformists believe that they can achieve this goal if the state merely takes up exploitation and then channels the profits made back to the workers in the form of "social institutions" and reforms.

The Bolsheviks tried to abolish the laws of movement of today's production system and to distribute the social product both through the enterprises and to the consumers *in natura*. This soon turned out to be impossible, and the above-mentioned reformist method was adopted. The result is the same in both cases: state capitalism.

d. Distribution of means of production and consumer goods in kind as a Bolshevik ideal[10]

The Bolsheviks had as their goal a situation in which wage labor and exploitation would be abolished. They purposefully aimed for the abolition of money, which was to come about through a massive "inflation" of the medium of exchange. The state printers worked day and night to print more and more paper money, which the state used for payments, but for which it did not guarantee any counter value.

»Notes are fabricated ... You can't print enough notes. The need for it is even greater than the possibility of fabrication.«[11]

With the increase in the total amount of "money" spent, the "exchange value", the purchasing power of the ruble, naturally declined. The prices of goods jumped daily, a phenomenon that we also know from the German inflation period. The "value" of the exchange medium declined so quickly that those who had something to sell no longer wanted to sell their goods for "money". They wanted to sell their

---

[10] See also Chapter 11 - The abolition of the market
[11] A. Goldschmidt, Wirtschaftsorgnisation in Sowjet-Russland (Economic Organization in Soviet Russia), p. 138

goods, but only directly against other goods, without using the intermediate form of money: they only wanted to exchange goods "in-kind".

This was just what the Bolsheviks wanted. In a commemorative document of the Russian Finance Commissariat, which was sent to all participants of the 3rd Congress of the III. International in 1921 in Moscow, *this policy of inflation is praised as a consciously applied method of introducing communism.*

This type of communism would then take such a form that the central economic council of the Soviet state would take control of the production and distribution of goods, eliminating money and trade. It would have to determine for all inhabitants how much bread, butter, clothes, etc. each individual can get, and assign them these goods in "Natura". This should be made possible by *conscientious production and consumption statistics.*

»The proletarian economy is, in principle, a commodity economy, an economy in kind. With the expansion of the state economy, first of all, the money disappears from the traffic between public enterprises. The coal mines supply the railways and ironworks with coal without any price settlement. The ironworks deliver the iron to the machine factories; these deliver the machines to the state agricultural enterprises without the mediation of the money. The workers receive an ever-larger

part of their wages in kind: housing, heating, bread, meat, etc ... Money also dies off as a means of circulation.«[12]

The production and distribution calculation would therefore not be done in money, or any other general measure, but only in sums of goods. One would calculate in kilograms, meters, tons, etc. or finally, only by the number of pieces of consumer goods. One would pass over with a word to the "natural economy", which is characterized by Otto Neurath as follows:

»The doctrine of the socialist economy knows only one single producer-distributor-society - who, without profit or loss account, without circulation of money - be it metal money or labor money - organizes production based on an economic plan, and distributes the standard of living according to socialist rules, **without** *foundation of* **any unit of account.**«[13]

From 1917 to 21, the Bolsheviks tried to realize this principle, and the commemorative document mentioned above is still to be regarded as a final extension of these attempts: In 1921, the ruble was stabilized and "stable money" was returned.

---

[12] Eugen Varga, Die wirtschaftspolitischen Probleme der proletarischen Diktatur (The economic problems of the proletarian dictatorship), p. 138
[13] Otto Neurath, Wirtschaftsplan und Naturalrechnung (Economic Plan and Calculation in Kind), p. 84

It was by no means the absence of the world revolution, nor was the individual peasant enterprise the reason why the Soviet state had to abandon its plans for "moneyless production and distribution" by calculating "in-kind" and had to stabilize the ruble. It only turned out that production and distribution on this "communist basis" were impossible.

The Russian Revolution practically proved that production without a unit of account is madness!

When trying to redirect the Russian economy, it was right to start from a predetermined plan. The individual operations made their budget plans, which were then processed by the central trust management into a general trust plan. The compilation of all trust plans gave the Supreme National Economic Council an overview of the entire production apparatus combined in the state, from which a general production plan for the entire state industry could be composed.

All these plans were <u>based on the calculation in rubles</u>. And why not on the calculation in "Natura"? Because you can't add up kilos of iron and tons of steel. However, the value of the ruble quickly decreased, and the prices of the products rose just as quickly. The budgets were, therefore, only on paper - they had no value for the real production process.

Varga, who acknowledges the merits of the "inflation method", finds its biggest downside in this. He says:

»*The rapid and continued devaluation of money is disadvantageous in so far as it prevents the stabilization of wage levels, causes wage movements and conflicts between the workers of the state and the proletarian state itself, forces them to constant wage increases, makes the calculation very difficult, makes it impossible to draw up a proper state budget, and especially to adhere to it.*«[14]

This is one of the practical reasons why the Soviet state had to refrain from destroying "stable money". Already in 1919, it was stated that »*the calculation of the value of the product becomes more necessary every day*« so that the 2nd Economic Congress (1919) already decided to »*calculate the most important state expenditures according to the value of the products*«. (Goldschmidt, p. 133). Of course, this is only possible if all production is based on value. The general stabilization of money, therefore, had to follow.

The stabilization of the ruble, therefore, meant that state capitalism, which was organized immediately

---

[14] Eugen Varga, Die wirtschaftspolitischen Probleme der proletarischen Diktatur (The economic problems of the proletarian dictatorship), p. 138

during the implementation of the revolution, stabilized its own laws of movement in the course of its development.

In the Russian economy, the means of industrial production passed into the hands of the state. The decision about it as well as about work (and thus about the workers) and about the work product lies in the hands of the Supreme National Economic Council.

The producers have no control over the product. The separation of work and labor product is the essential characteristic of the production.

The Supreme National Economic Council can control production only based on the *value of the products*. It must therefore also calculate the *value of the labor power*; it must give the worker, in exchange for his labor power, as much right to the social product as the value of the labor power is. That is his reward. The workers are, therefore, wage laborers.

The Supreme Economic Council must buy the labor power on the market using the method of the collective agreement with the trade unions, which is also used in Western capitalism.

e. Wage Labor and State Communism

Firstly, it is important to realize that production based on the value of the labor power, i.e., **wage labor**, can never lead to anything other than the disenfranchisement of workers. The reason for this lies not in the badness of the state administrators, but in the laws of movement of the system.

The crucial point is that there is a contradiction between the value of the labor power and **the work** that the worker delivers daily to his boss. We are never paid for our **work**, but in exchange for our work, we get as much as is necessary to maintain the necessary livelihood.[15]

With our wages, we take every week several goods from the market in which, for example, no more than 24 hours of social work is involved. In reality, we have worked 40, 50, 60, or more hours this week. **The work** that we give to society in this way more than we get from our wages is called **extra work**, which then represents **a surplus value** for the owners of the means of production or the state. The lower the wages and the longer the working day, the greater the surplus value that goes to the state or the capitalists.

---

[15] See: chapter 7 g., The Value of Labor in Capitalism According to Marx

Mistakenly, there is a widespread opinion that the creation of surplus-value is good in itself, but that this surplus value should not belong to the owning class, but should be returned to the workers by the communist state through social legislation.

This view is wrong because it does not consider the social importance of wage labor.

We have already pointed out that there is a contrast between **the value of the labor power** and day-to-day **work**. The peculiarity is that the amount of **work** we give to society has nothing to do with the number of goods we take from the market through our wages. In other words, there is no direct connection between the wealth of goods we produce and our wages. The worker does **not** determine his share of the product through his work.

Not our **work**, but the *value of our labor power* determines which part of the wealth of goods we will receive.

From the point of view of the wage earner, his share of the national product is thus practically a blow to the air. His wage will fluctuate around the value of the labor power, but he will have to fight for it, regardless of whether it is a capitalist or a "communist" *state*. Because facts speak better than the grey theory, we will demonstrate this later in the light of Russian experience.

The peculiarity that the amount of **work** we give to society has nothing to do with wages is much more important than the question of distribution alone. This means that the wage-worker has nothing to do with the social product. It is an expression of the fact that the producer is separated from the social product. It means

*That the producer has **nothing** to do with the management and administration of the social production process.*

This is the essential meaning of a production in which the labor power is paid based on value!

It also means social antagonisms within the working class, social antagonisms between the workers and the "red directors" of the factories. It means the struggle of the workers against "their" state.

*The **value** of the **labor power** is the bearer of all these conflicts.*

This is because **our work** does **not** determine our relationship to the social product!

The workers, who believe that a communist revolution is only about passing on the surplus-value of the owners to the state, are therefore deeply mistaken.

Basically, the workers want to rearrange their relationship to the social product in a communist production. And they think they have built a new relationship when they exclude the capitalists from the surplus value in order to let it flow to the state. What is actually happening is a new distribution of surplus-value in society. But what does this mean for wage earners? There is no new relationship between producer and social product. In capitalism, this relationship was determined by the value of the labor power and in so-called "communism" ... *also*. For the wage workers, therefore, the goal of the proletarian revolution can only be to establish a **new relationship between the producer and the social product**.

For the proletarian, the goal of social revolution can be no other than to determine through his **work** at the same time his relationship to the social product. This means:

Abolition of wage labor!

Work is the measure of consumption!

It is the only condition for putting the management and administration of social production in the hands of the workers themselves.

When the Russians began to operate production based on value, they proclaimed the expropriation of the workers from the means of production, and they proclaimed that there was no direct connection between the wealth of the goods to be produced and the share of the workers in the social product.

All capitalist elements thus crept into the economy as soon as **value** and **surplus-value** resumed their ordering work. It is the secret force that works everywhere and cannot be grasped concretely anywhere that controls social life with an invisible hand.

That is why Lenin had to sigh:

»The machine refused to obey the hand that guided it. It was like a car that was going not in the direction the driver desired, but in the direction someone else desired; as if it were being driven by some mysterious, lawless hand, God knows whose, perhaps of a profiteer, or of a private capitalist, or of both. Be that as it may, the car is not going quite in the direction the man at the wheel imagines, and often it goes in an altogether different direction. (...) I doubt very much whether it can truthfully be said that the Communists are directing that heap. To tell the truth, they are not directing, they are being directed.«[16]

The value of the labor power "orders" the wages:

---

[16] W. I. Lenin, Eleventh Congress Of The R.C.P.(B.), Political Report Of The Central Committee Of The R.C.P. (B.) March 27. March 1922, in: Works, Vol. 33. P. 279 / 288

"The foreign visitors are amazed at nothing as much as at the wage differences between educated and unskilled workers that in Russia ... are bigger as nowhere else in Western Europe."[17]

Next, we want to illustrate how the struggle not to let wages fall below the value of the labor power continued in Russia:

»While the communist in the capitalist countries must support the wage demands, he cannot do so under the proletarian dictatorship. ... Here the economic demands of the workers must be reconciled with the development of the productive forces and socialist accumulation. When the wage demands were raised in July (1926), none of the trade unions supported these demands. The Central Council of Trade Unions could not support them ... because there had been a price increase since spring. ... Under these circumstances, the demand for a wage increase meant that the actual wage had to be adjusted when the price rose. But that would mean official recognition of the decline in monetary value ... and we couldn't comment on that.«[18]

---

[17] Tomski - at the 7th Congress of Trade Unions. A closer look at the wage movement can be found in the brochure "De Beweging van het kapitalistisch Bedrijfsleven", second chapter "The Marixist wage laws". Edition of the G.I.C. (Holland)

[18] Tomski - 7th Congress of Trade Unions, Protokol p. 49. translated from Dutch, English version unknown

In 1921 the calculation according to value was introduced. The prices of goods rose. In 1921 the index of retail prices was 139, and in 1922 – 98. Since the **work** of the worker has nothing to do with the wealth of the goods produced, wages lagged far behind price increases. As a result, there were major strikes to prevent the price of the labor power from falling too much below its value. These strikes were almost all "wild" strikes, and only in a few cases, to the great annoyance of the central unions, were supported by the local unions. The trade union organ "Voprocy Truda" 1924 No. 7/8 provides the following information on this subject, although the editorial staff notes that the statistics are not complete:

In 1921, 477 strikes were carried out with 184,000 strikers.

In 1922 there were 505 strikes with 154,000 strikers.

95 % of the strikers belonged to state enterprises. Of all these strikes, only 11 were supported by the unions. Dogadov then provided the following information at the 7th Trade Union Congress:

In 1924 there were 267 strikes, 151 of them in state-owned enterprises.

In 1925 there were 199 strikes, 99 of them in state-owned enterprises.

The unions supported none of these strikes.

The fact that the unions did not support these wage movements is, of course, because they were incorporated into the state apparatus. At the 11th Congress of the CPR (March-April 1922), trade unionist Andreyev acknowledged "the difficult material condition of the workers" but complained that the unions "make excessive wage demands on the state and demand from it as much as possible". Andreyev declared that various unions support the wage demands because former Mensheviks and Social Revolutionaries permeate the trade union apparatus. This was followed by a "cleansing" of the trade union apparatus.

Production based on the value of the labor power determines that workers have nothing to do with the administration and management of production.

From Russian experience:

»... with the urgent necessity to increase labor productivity, to work lossless, and to achieve profitability of each enterprise ... inevitably leads to a certain contradiction of interests between the working masses and the directors, heads of state enterprises or authorities to which these enterprises are subordinate in questions of working conditions in the enterprise. Therefore,

concerning socialized enterprises, trade unions have an unconditional duty to defend the interests of the workers ...«.[19]

This was indeed necessary because the Central Council of Trade Unions stated that the Supreme National Economic Council was »*not guided by the interests of workers, but by the financial interests of industry*« in the area of occupational health and safety. ("Trud" - 1928, No. 31)

This meant that the Supreme Economic Council did not provide sufficient funds for occupational health and safety in enterprises. But the "red directors" made it even better. They used only a small part of the seemingly scarce funds for occupational safety. They probably put the rest into the company. For example, the "Trud" - 1928, No. 32 - gives the following figures:

The Ukrainian state trust consumed 20 %. It is, therefore, likely that 80% of the funds earmarked for health and safety at work were invested in companies. The Urals Asbestos Trust consumed only

---

[19] The role and tasks of trade unions under the conditions of the New Economic Policy, Resolution of the XI Party Congress CPR March-April 1922
http://www.verlag-benario-baum.de/WebRoot/Store/Shops/es151175/MediaGallery/PDF-Dateien/Die_KPdSU_in_Resolutionen_und_Beschluessen_Band_2.pdf

28%, the Donugol 18.7%, the Yugosteel 14.8%, and the Jushni-Rudnit Trust, only 4.9%. In fact, economic management!

The consequences were inevitable: **Accidents at work** ("Trud", 1928, No. 159)

In the Donugol Trust, 1925 - 18.7% of all workers had an accident; in 1926, it was 26.3% or 18,821 men. In 1927 it rose to 25,749 men.

The number of accidents in the coal and steel industry:

1923 11.5%

1925 18%

1926 25%

Finally, some data from the "Trud", 1928, No. 280.

The number of accidents in mining 1927/1928:

October-December 1927 - 8.3%.

January-March 1928 - 9.3%

April-June 1928 - 10%.

The number of accidents, therefore, rose by around 1% each quarter. In the metal industry, the number of accidents in the same period was 6.8%, 7.1%, and 7.9%, respectively. Here, too, there was a regular increase.

<u>This is the regulating function of value and surplus-value!</u>

We want to leave it at that. For us, it is only a matter of seeing these things from a certain perspective. And here it is that in Russia this procedure cannot be attributed to the malice of the Russian state administrators, but that it is a necessary consequence of a production in which the labor power appears as a commodity, regardless of whether a state buys this labor power or a private entrepreneur. Nor does it have anything to do with whether the surplus-value is created for private individuals or for the state. **The value** performs its function of order. And then you have to say with Lenin:

»I doubt very much whether it can truthfully be said that the Communists are directing that heap. To tell the truth, they are not directing, they are being directed.«[20]

---

[20] W. I. Lenin, Eleventh Congress Of The R.C.P.(B.), Political Report Of The Central Committee Of The R.C.P. (B.) March 27. March 1922, in: works, vol. 33. P. 288

3.
The unit of account in communism

a. The regulation of production

In the "Marxist explanation of the domination of the working class", we have seen that the real problem of communism lies in abolishing the separation of labor and labor product. It is not some Supreme Economic Council, but the producers *themselves*, who must have the disposal of the work product through their operational organizations. Only in this way can they become free producers, and can then group themselves in mutual connection to the associations of free and equal producers. Since today's technology has socialized the whole production, all operations *are* technically completely dependent on each other, and together form an uninterrupted working process, it is the task of the revolution to forge them *economically* together. But this is only possible if *a general economic law* unifies the whole economic process.

This association is of a completely different nature than the so-called "socialization theories" describe it. These have never had anything else in mind, but the *organizational* merger of the different branches of production. They deal with the question, *which* industries have to be united and how the problem is solved organizationally and technically. This has nothing to do with the laws of movement of a new economic system. The new general economic law, which unites the entire economic process, therefore says nothing about the organizational unification of the economy. It only establishes the conditions under which the producers, united in the operational organizations, participate in the great general economic process. These conditions must, first of all, be the same for each part of the total process. In contrast to Lenin, who starts from the principle:

»To organize the whole economy on the lines of the postal service ... that is our immediate aim«,[21]

We say:

Equal economic conditions for all parts of social production that is our first demand.

Only then the question of the technique of organization can be addressed.

The same economic conditions primarily relate to the implementation of a generally binding fixed measure, according to which all calculations are car-

---

[21] W. I. Lenin. State and Revolution, works 25, p. 432

ried out in production and distribution. This measure can no longer be money because no "third person" inserts himself between the worker and his product. Here the worker is not "alienated" from the social product of labor. Indeed, the worker does not directly consume the product produced by himself. Still, his product has something in it that all social goods have in common: the socially necessary working time that cost their production. All goods are, therefore, qualitatively completely equal *from a social point of view*. They differ only in the amount of social work they have absorbed in the production process.

Just as the benchmark for individual working time is the working hour, the measure for the amount of social work contained in the products must be the *socially average working hour*.

Thus, as a compelling demand of the proletarian revolution, it turns out that all operational organizations are obliged to calculate for the products produced by them how much socially average working time they have taken up in production, and at the same time to pass on their product according to this "price" to the other operations or to the consumers. Furthermore, the operational organizations receive the same amount of social work in the form of other products in order to be able to continue the production process in the same way. In this way, all participate in the production process under the same economic conditions. If this regulation of distribution and production is carried out, then the whole economic life, which is already socially *connected* by the division of labor, is now also economically, i.e., socially *regulated*.

Capitalism tries to implement this regulation by organizational means by increasing the concentration of its power in the industry. What it succeeds in doing is only to organize the competition at an ever-higher level, with ever greater catastrophes in the wake. It tries politically, according to the rules of "democracy", to achieve a mildness of opposites, but this ultimately serves only to organize the last and deepest opposition, that between the owning class and the proletariat, and to secure its continued existence. This social condition can only be overcome if the workers make themselves "free"; if they conquer the right of disposal over the means of production and participate in the economic process under equal economic conditions.

However, the revolution does not only consist of a revolution of the economic conditions of production, but it also brings new economic conditions for individual consumption. If the workers have the right of disposal over the work product in their hands, then their relationship to this product must be *determined and regulated* on a new basis. For the workers do have the right of disposal over the product, but no longer in the sense of private capitalism with *arbitrarily free disposal*. The disposal of the product can only take place under social and equal conditions. Producers and consumers are indeed free, but only through their social ties. The same conditions for individual consumption can, in turn, only lie within the same measure of consumption. Just as the individual working hour is the measure of individual work, the individual working hour is also the measure of individual consumption. Consumption is thus also *socially regulated* and moves in completely exact tracks.

The implementation of the social revolution is thus in essence nothing other than the implementation of the working hour as a measure in the entire economic life. It serves as a measure in production, and at the same time, it measures the producers' right to social products.

The essential thing, however, is that this category is carried out by the producers and consumers themselves.

And this does not happen because it is an "ethical" or "moral" demand of communism, but because it is economically not otherwise possible. In fact, the "emancipation of labor", the development and flourishing of free man, is also an ethical demand.

But this only proves once more that the economy and ethics can only realize each other; - they become both merged into unity.

b. The socially average working time by Marx and Engels

In our analysis of the conditions of communist production and distribution we started from the Marxist analysis of the domination of the working class and, as mentioned above, we did not hold on to quotations, because they never prove the correctness of a view, but at most can clarify a representation. For those of us who find "serious anarchist deviations", we want to confront our view with that of Marx and Engels. It will become apparent that these "deviations" were their essential view of communist society.

In this context, it should also be noted that the Bolshevik stupidity of producing goods without a 'unit of account' is a completely foreign element for Marx and Engels.

Engels clearly states the socially average working time as a unit of account:

»Society can simply calculate how many hours of labor are contained in a steam-engine, a bushel of wheat of the last harvest, or a hundred square yards of cloth of a certain quality. It could therefore never occur to it still to express the quantities

of labor put into the products, quantities which it will then know directly and in their absolute amounts, in a third product, in a measure which, besides, is only relative, fluctuating, inadequate, though formerly unavoidable for lack of a better one, rather than express them in their natural, adequate and absolute measure, **time** *... Hence, on the assumptions we made above, society will not assign values to products.«*[22]

Marx also very clearly states the working hour as the arithmetic unit. At the discussion of the well-known "Robinson on the island", he says of this island inhabitant, who built himself his entire economic life:

»The need itself forces him to distribute his time exactly between his different functions. Whether the one takes up more and the other less space in his overall activity depends on the greater or lesser difficulty to be overcome in order to achieve the intended effect. Experience teaches him this, and our Robinson, who rescued the clock, ledger, ink, and pen from the shipwreck, soon begins to keep a record of himself as a good Englishman. His inventory contains a list of all the utensils he possesses, the various tasks he has been called upon to perform in order to produce them, and, finally, the working time that certain Quanta of these various products cost him on average. All the relations between Robinson and the things

---

[22] F. Engels, Anti-Dühring, Part III: Socialism, IV. Distribution

that make up his self-created wealth are so simple and transparent here that even Mr. M. Wirth should be able to understand them without any particular mental effort.«[23]

»*Let us finally, for a change, imagine an association of free people who work with social means of production and self-confidently spend their many individual labor power as a social labor power. All the provisions of Robinson's work are repeated here, only socially instead of individually.*«[24]

We see here that Marx also knows a production calculation for "an association of free people", and that *on the basis of the working hour.*

Where Marx replaces Robinson with free people, we now want to read society's accounting as follows:

Its inventory contains a list of the articles of daily use that it owns, the various activities that it is engaged in its production, finally, *the working hours that certain quanta of these various products cost* it on average. All relationships between members of society and things here are so simple that anyone can grasp them.

Marx accepts this bookkeeping of society *in general* for a production process with common means of

---

[23] Karl Marx, Capital Volume 1, p. 91
[24] Karl Marx, Capital Volume 1, p. 92

production; thus, whether communism is still "little" developed or whether it has already reached its highest development. This means that economic life in communism can go through various stages of development, but the category of *average social working time remains the dormant pole.*

If we now come to the individual distribution of the social product, then as Marx, we also see working hours as a measure of individual consumption:

»We will assume, but merely for the sake of a parallel with the production of commodities, that the share of each individual producer in the means of subsistence is determined by his labor time. Labor time would, in that case, play a double part. Its apportionment in accordance with a definite social plan maintains the proper proportion between the different kinds of work to be done and the various wants of the community. On the other hand, it also serves as a measure of the portion of the common labor borne by each individual, and of his share in the part of the total product destined for individual consumption. The social relations of the individual producers, with regard both to their labor and to its products, are in this case perfectly simple and intelligible, and that with regard not only to production but also to distribution.«[25]

---

[25] Karl Marx, Capital Vol. 1, p. 51. Highlighting by GIC

Elsewhere, too, it can be seen that Marx sees working time as a basic category of the communist economy:

»*In the case of socialized production, the money-capital is eliminated. Society distributes labor-power and means of production to the different branches of production. The producers may, for all it matters, receive paper vouchers entitling them to withdraw from the social supplies of consumer goods a quantity corresponding to their labor-time. These vouchers are not money. They do not circulate.*«[26]

The entire communist economy is included in these sentences! If the individual working time is to be the *measure* for the product to be consumed individually, then the product mass must also be measured with the same measure. In other words: the products must express how much human labor, measured by time, how many socially average working hours they contain. This presupposes, however, that the other categories of production (means of production, raw and auxiliary materials) are measured with the same measure, so that the entire production calculation in the operations must be based on the socially average working hour!

However, it should be noted that Marx did not raise the distribution issue in absolute terms, but gave the

---

[26] Karl Marx, Capital Volume 2, p. 218

impression that another distribution method would indeed be possible:

»*The producers may, for all it matters, receive paper vouchers ...*«,

or in terms of working time:

»*merely for the sake of a parallel with the production of commodities.*«

If one takes the measure of individual consumption, it seems that there is a "free choice" of the distribution system. Marxistically, however, this is by no means the case. The reason for this "ambiguity" lies in the fact that Marx saw full-fledged communism as a "take as needed", with working time not being the measure of individual consumption. This measure would only be valid *for the transitional period* from capitalism to mature communism. This is clearly expressed in the *Critique of the Gotha Program*.

This also sheds light on the "Marxism" of those who see state capitalism as a form of transition to communism.

»*What we have to deal with here is a communist society, not as it has **developed** on its own foundations, but, on the contrary, just as it **emerges** from capitalist society [highlighted by Marx]; which is thus in every respect, economically, morally, and intellectually, still stamped with the birth-*

marks of the old society from whose womb it emerges. Accordingly, the individual producer receives back from society – after the deductions have been made – exactly what he gives to it. What he has given to it is his individual quantum of labor. For example, the social working day consists of the sum of the individual hours of work; the individual labor time of the individual producer is the part of the social working day contributed by him, his share in it. He receives a certificate from society that he has furnished such-and-such an amount of labor (after deducting his labor for the common funds); and with this certificate, he draws from the social stock of means of consumption as much as the same amount of labor cost. The same amount of labor which he has given to society in one form, he receives back in another.«[27]

»*In a higher phase of communist society, after the enslaving subordination of the individual to the division of labor, and therewith also the antithesis between mental and physical labor, has vanished; after labor has become not only a means of life but life's prime want; after the productive forces have also increased with the all-around development of the individual, and all the springs of co-operative wealth flow more abundantly – only then can the narrow horizon of bourgeois right be crossed in its entirety and society inscribe on its banners: From each according to his ability, to each according to his needs!*«[28]

---

[27] Karl Marx, Critique of the Gotha Programme
[28] Karl Marx, Critique of the Gotha Programme

4.
Progress in the formulation of the problem

a. Communism as a "negative system"

After this preliminary orientation on our topic, in which we have identified as characteristics of communist operational life the *self-management* by the operational organizations with an exact relationship from producer to product based on working time accounting, it is important to examine how the Bolsheviks developed their dream image of production without a "unit of account". It should be noted, however, that this was by no means a specific Bolshevik view, but dominated the entire working class, from the Social Democrats to the anarchists. Admittedly, they did not all talk openly about it, nor did it lead to a direct struggle against the position. In truth, this means that the workers' movement was not yet ready!

Part of the English labor movement is an exception, as English trade unionists made attempts before 1914 in the direction of so-called "guild socialism." Judging by its name, it gives the impression that England, which had always lagged far behind in socialist theory, went far beyond the mainland movement on these issues. However, the explanation for the case lies in the fact that the English trade unions were already stuck before 1914 in their task of "improving working conditions". They took no further steps and had to look for "other means". Certainly, no one will expect English trade unionists to launch a revolutionary attack on the capitalist system. Guild socialism" is, therefore, nothing more than the English name for the cooperation of capital and labor, as it is understood here in the country under "worker participation".

No matter how ridiculous it may be in retrospect, it is in any case explainable that it was believed that communism could be achieved without a unit of account. It was assumed that capitalism itself had to develop into such a state. And those who immediately saw the stupidity of such a view thought it completely superfluous to get lost in "utopias" because these things would, of course, find their solution by themselves.

In fact, there is always a solution by *itself*!

But since we know that the abolition of private ownership of the means of production, the transformation of the means of production into "common ownership" does not necessarily lead to communism, we believe that we cannot ignore this problem.

For those Marxists who consider any further investigation of the laws of the movement of communist operational life superfluous, who see in such an investigation only the resurrection of a refuted position, a relapse into utopian socialism, we recall the great scientific deed of Marx and Engels who, on the contrary, led communism from utopia to science. The realization of communism does not depend on benevolent people who will realize a predetermined "plan", who have "worked out" a certain production system in which all the evils of capitalism are eliminated. It must develop with natural necessity from the laws of movement of capital. Capitalism digs its own grave. The accumulation of capital, the condition of existence of the present system, is, at the same time, the precondition of its dying.

The accumulation of capital means only the accumulation of the misery of the working class, which confronts us with the choice of abolishing the laws of movement of the production of commodities, of the profitability of capital, by realizing communism or sinking into barbarism.

The impoverishment of the masses is nothing more than an expression of the fact that productive social forces have come into conflict with property relations so that they can no longer be applied within the framework of private property. The productive forces thus go beyond the ownership, through which the means of production are transferred into common ownership. Then communism will be there!

So why bother to examine the laws of the movement of communist production? Why supplement the existing utopias with another one? Why should Marxism develop from science to utopia?

But the propaganda demanded a more detailed explanation of the coming new order. The bourgeois critics did not stop asking again and again what the new order would look like so that theorists were forced to lift some of the mysterious veils. With a contemptuous shrug, they explained that communism was crystal clear for them.

Marx taught it:

»*The money disappears in communist production.*«

And beyond that, they had read that the work itself, although it is a value-forming element, cannot have any value itself, that therefore also

»*... a given quantity of work cannot have a value expressed in its price, in its equivalence with a given quantity of money.*«[29]

---

[29] Karl Marx, Capital Volume 2, p. 18

Accordingly, Kautsky explained:

»Value is the historical category that applies only to the production of commodities.«[30]

This would also abolish the "prices" of products, not to mention the "market".

When asked what the communist operational life would look like, the Marxist economists were able to give a very satisfactory answer to their feelings. However, this was in fact not an answer. They always said what it would not be like: **no money, no value, no market, no price**.

The bourgeois writer Erich Horn, who would very much like to know what it will be like, therefore characterizes communism as *«a negative system"*.[31]

His curiosity was awakened because he concluded that he might also be a communist! He has no objection at all to the abolition of private ownership of the means of production, he is, if necessary, in favor of leaving them to "common ownership," but that in no way meant *the abolition of the capitalist mode of production*![32]

---

[30] Karl Kautsky, Karl Marx` Ökonomische Lehren, p. 20
[31] E. Horn, Die ökonomische Grenzen der Gemeinwirtschaft, p. 3
[32] As above, p. 51 and 52

b. The General Cartel of Hilferding

Rudolf Hilferding deserves the dubious honor of having given the complacent superficiality of the "negative system" a "theoretical" basis. He solved the difficulties in a surprisingly simple way, so simple that a child can understand the movement of the new production system.

Hilferding pointed out that the money-capital destroys *itself* in the course of the capitalist development because the ever-stronger concentration of enterprises and industries makes money and the clearing between the individual enterprises redundant, in his opinion. The trusts create huge industrial hubs in which transport, coal and iron mines, steel mills, etc., and even the distribution of the final product to consumers, are organized, managed, and controlled in one hand. In this huge apparatus, the products for continuous processing go from one company to another without being "sold" every time, because the trust does not sell anything to itself.

Within the trust, the money movement (according to Hilferding!) has stopped. Yes, the products in the individual companies no longer even have a "price": *Within its production cycle, the Trust has switched over to the production of goods "in-kind"*. In order to regulate production within the trust, the top trust management decides in which plant and how many new means of production are added and what and how much is produced in the individual plants.

This is an amazingly simple solution for communist economic life! The more capital is organized in trusts, the more capital itself destroys money, the greater the extent to which society goes to the account "in-kind". After all, it would theoretically turn out that the entire world production is an awesome monster trust in which production and distribution are deliberately regulated, but on a capitalist basis! This means that the owners of the monster trust let the entire apparatus work for their private purposes. But here the money has disappeared, money is no longer there, prices and the "market" do not exist. The trust leaders would set prices for the distribution of consumer goods to the workers, but these would in no way be related to the "value": They would have been set arbitrarily according to the standards set by the gentlemen.

Hilferding tells the following about this monster trust or, as he calls it, the "<u>General Cartel</u>":

»All capitalist production is consciously regulated by an authority that determines the extent of production in all spheres. Then the price-fixing becomes purely nominal (here: arbitrary - G.I.C.) and means only the distribution of the total product to the cartel magnates on the one hand, to the mass of all other

members of society on the other hand. The price is then not the result of a factual relationship that people have entered into, but merely of a calculated way of allocating things from people to people. Money does not matter then. It can disappear completely because it is about the allocation of things and not of values. With the anarchy of production, the material appearance disappears, the value of the commodities disappears, and thus money disappears. The cartel distributes the product. The objective production elements have been produced again and used for new production. Of the new production, one part is distributed to the working class and the intellectuals, the other part falls to the cartel, for any use. It is the consciously regulated society in antagonistic form. But this antagonism is an antagonism of distribution. The distribution itself is consciously regulated, and thus the need for money is over. The financial capital in its completion is detached from the breeding ground in which it was created. The circulation of money has become unnecessary; the restless circulation of money has reached its goal; the regulated society and the perpetual mobile of circulation finds its rest.»[33]

When the "Marxist economists" had read this, they looked at each other very meaningfully through their glasses. Yes, yes, Marx was right that capitalism was digging its own grave and that a new society was

---

[33] Rudolf Hilferding, Das Finanzkapital, Wien 1920 (Finance Capital), p. 314
www.marxists.org/archive/hilferding/1910/finkap/

born in the womb of the old. Any further trustification means another step towards the self-destruction of capital! And how simple communism was!

The working class only had to remove the obstacles of private ownership of the means of production that prevented the implementation of the "General Cartel", in order to unite all economic life in one hand and thus create the communist system in which there would be **no money**, **no market**, **no value,** and **no prices**.

The fact that it is still necessary to measure by each individual product how much work it embodies was obviously an error by Marx and Engels, which was probably connected with their simple line of thought about the "association of free and equal producers". But in the end, they had to be forgiven for this, because they lived in the heyday of capital and had therefore not experienced the enormous formation of trusts and monopolies.

Upon closer inspection, Marx's whole formulation that capitalism was digging its own grave was based on a misunderstanding, because this grave-digger work had a completely different meaning for Marx!

For Marx, it digs its own grave because the capital that flows into the means of production is growing ever faster. At the same time, the number of workers who have to produce surplus-value is constantly decreasing proportionally. Finally, this creates a point at which the profitability of capital becomes impossible so that the system collapses under terrible crises. There are then large, operational factory complexes, but the workers are superfluous by the millions because capital does not yield a profit.

For the disciples of Marx, digging the grave is much more comfortable. Here "Stinnes is the greatest socialist" (this expression was indeed used in "Vorwärts"! Unfortunately, we do not know in what number) and leads the organization of capitalism "gradually" into communism.

We must refrain here from a value-theoretical criticism of the "General Cartel", since this is not directly related to our topic. We only wanted to show how the "General Cartel" was theoretically justified, how the generally accepted view of communism came about.

We find a very good critique based on the value theory in: H. Grossmann »Law of the Accumulation and Breakdown«.[34]

Following this theoretical foundation of communism, where there would be no money, no market, no value, and no prices, the practical side was

---

[34] Das Akkumulations- und Zusammenbruchsgesetz des kapitalistischen Systems, Leipzig, 1929, p. 603

only a question of organization. It was the conversion of the apparatus to the needs of the people, a conversion that the leaders of production and distribution had to make. The state officials had to compile precise statistics on the needs, at which point the central management would ensure that the products were manufactured and distributed to the workers. Therefore, it was important:

»How, where, how much, by what means, will new products be made from the available natural and artificial production conditions ... the communal, district and national commissioners of socialist society decide, overseeing social needs by all means of organized production and consumption statistics, consciously foreseeing the whole economic life according to the needs of their consciously represented and directed communities.«[35]

The Russian Revolution has put an end to this beautiful dream! The factories were converted into "common property", the Hilferdings "General Cartel" was implemented in the state industry, but it did not abolish the movement laws of capital. The central trust administration must buy the labor power on the market at a price stipulated in the collective labor agreements with the state unions.

The Russian Revolution made a thick line through the blessings of the "General Cartel" and forced us

---

[35] Rudolf Hilferding, Finance Capital, S. 1

to examine more closely the laws of movement of the communist economic world.

c. The bourgeois criticism of the "General Cartel"

The development of science, which deals with the communist economy, thus does not show a straight line. Still, from the working time calculation of Marx and Engels, it turns to the calculation "in-kind", to be brought back to its old course around 1920.

It is certainly a bitter irony that bourgeois economists, in particular, have made good progress in the science of communism, unless unintentionally. When it appeared that the downfall of capitalism had come within reach and communism seemed to conquer the world by storm, Max Weber and Ludwig Mises began their criticism of this communism, whereby of course first and foremost Hilferding's "General Cartel", that is Russian communism, had to suffer. Their criticism culminated in the demonstration that *an economy is impossible without a method of accounting, without a general denominator to measure the value of the products.*

And they had it right! Great confusion in the "Marxist" camp. It was perfectly clear that the chaos of capitalist production was an orderly system compared to the "production of goods" without a unit of account.

Only a small part of the Social Democrats held on to the old love (Neurath), while the majority recognized the need for a general measure in economic life. Kautsky, too, was shocked and now had to deviate from his old method of ignoring something with a pretext and "take a stand". That's what he does. The value is now suddenly no longer a "historical category" because the "settlement" will take place *based on money*, since it is *»indispensable as a measure of value for bookkeeping and the calculation of exchange ratios in a socialist society«*[36] and also *»as a means of circulation«*. What money will look like in the "second phase" of communism is an open question for him, for we do not even know *»whether it will ever be more than a pious wish, similar to the Millennial Kingdom«*.[37]

Weber and Mises had won the battle: Communism was defeated. But now they still had to deal with Marx and Engels, because they had never participated in the stupidity of production without a unit of account, but had set the working time as a measure. They did this so thoroughly that Bloch, in his

---

[36] Karl Kautsky, Die proletarische Revolution und ihr Programm (The proletarian revolution and its program), p. 318
[37] Karl Kautsky, as above, p. 317

"Die Marxsche Geldtheorie," p. 125, considered it unnecessary to go into the details of the working time calculation.

In fact, no part of the working time calculation remained intact, but only because they understood so much, or rather so little about this matter as Kautsky did: nothing at all!

The first fruit of Weber's criticism was the outstanding work of Otto Leichter, The economic account in the socialist community (Die Wirtschaftrechnung in der Sozialistischen Gesellschaft, Vienna, 1923).

Because he based production on the working time accounting, communism made a great leap forward here. He wants to place production in the hands of the producers, but because he cannot or does not want to implement the category of socially average production time, the matter nevertheless leads to state capitalism.

We also learn from his writing that he was not the first to base production on working time accounting. This way of thinking was not only developed by Marx but around 1900 also by Maurice Bourquin, whose thoughts, according to Leichter's explanation, "almost exactly match" his own.

Besides, several people make working time play an important role in the production, but since *none of them includes the means of production* in their calculations, they lead nowhere. Also, the explanation of Varga in Kommunismus, 2nd year no. 9/10 suffers from this lack. Therefore this also does not have to be considered with further investigation.

d. The progress

However, progress in the formulation of the problem is revealed not only from the economic side but also from the "political" side. The revolutionary proletariat has already pointed out that the production apparatus can be "social property," while it continues to function as an apparatus of domination and exploitation. Thus, the Russian revolution has posed the problems from the political side. We now demand *guarantees* that we will retain the right to decide on the means of production. That is why we are now calling for *generally applied rules* on how producers themselves manage and administer production, with precise controls to ensure that these rules are actually applied.

The type of syndicalism that seeks "free" disposal of operation must, therefore, be seriously combated.

In addition to the guarantees for maintaining the right of disposal over the production apparatus, we are now also demanding *guarantees* that exploitation will actually be abolished. And these guarantees cannot lie in "democracy", in influencing the "leading instances" on the path of elections for all kinds of councils. We demand this guarantee over the objective course of the production and distribution apparatus, which goes beyond every democracy:

We demand an exact relationship between the producer and the social product as a whole!

The basis for these guarantees lies in the fact that it is:

»necessary for society to know how much labor each article of consumption requires for its production.«[38]

That is its: **production time**!

And so, we have come to a very clear objective for our further research: We must examine how the category of the *socially average production time* is developing in the communist economy.

Our paper will continue to be dedicated to this topic. So, we are by no means constructing a "vision of the future". We are not "inventing" a "communist system". We only examine the conditions under which the central category - the average

---

[38] Frederick Engels, Anti-Dühring, Part III: Socialism, IV. Distribution
www.marxists.org/archive/marx/works/1877/anti-duhring/

working hour in society - can be introduced. If this is not possible, then the exact relationship of producer to total product can no longer be maintained, then the distribution is no longer determined by the objective course of the production apparatus, then we get a distribution *by persons to persons*, then producers and consumers can no longer determine the course of the operational life, but then this is shifted to the dictatorial power of the "central organs", then the state enters the operational life *with* "democracy", then state capitalism is inevitable.

5.
Libertarian communism

a. "Occupy the enterprises", "Take as needed"

It is sad to note it, but it is hardly worth the effort to look at the different factions within the labor movement in terms of their views on communist operational life. It is an infertile wasteland of uniformity.

In all currents, we find the *same economic principles*, which are represented only in different phrases. Social democracy, Bolshevism, syndicalism, the cross between "Marxism" and syndicalism, which we call guild socialism, anarchism: it's all from one mold.

If we leave the social-democratic worker's movement for the time being to look more closely at "libertarian communism" (syndicalism and anarchism), the federalist structure of this movement immediately catches the eye. From this, it can be directly deduced that the communist economy is also understood here as a federal summary of producers and consumers. This direction is therefore strongly directed against the state, while *self*-management is one of its characteristic features.

Although there is no well-founded economic theory of libertarian communism, the general way of thinking that exists among the workers can be summarized briefly.

Basically, the "theory" does not go beyond the slogan: "*The enterprises to the workers*". The reciprocal relationship between the companies is "regulated" by the "*free agreement*", and what the relationship between the producers and the social product will look like, we hear the vaguest rumors about that. It is partly assumed that enterprises will become productive associations, in which the workers will then distribute "the proceeds of labor", and part of the idea is that enterprises, through the "free agreement", will enter into a direct trade in goods and simply deliver their product to the place where it is requested, without charging. Another characteristic of libertarian communism is that it often manages to solve the question of individual consumption quite simply with the formula, "*Everyone takes according to his needs!*".

Although libertarian communism seems quite close to the Marxist association of free and equal producers due to the *demand for self-government*, this is by no means the case. In this camp, there is no idea what *free* producers and *equal* producers are. In libertarian communism, the slogan "The enterprises to the workers" has the meaning that the workers regard the enterprises as their "property", which they can arbitrarily dispose of. In the Marxist sense, however, the new legal relationship is that the operations belong to the *community*. Machines and raw materials are *social goods* controlled by the workers and entrusted to the workers responsible for production management. This directly means that the *community must also have control* over the proper management of its products. However, libertarian communism firmly rejects such control, since the workers are then again "no bosses in their own house".

We also find this ideological contradiction *in the free agreement*. Communism does not know this category. It only knows *equal* producers, equal, because they *have to* run their business according to generally binding rules. *Only on this basis* can they make connections with other companies. The so-called "free agreement" contradicts any generally applicable social regulation and is therefore anti-communist.

b. Libertarian state capitalism

The weakness of the so-called libertarian communism becomes immediately visible as soon as its representatives begin to elaborate on their "fundamental principles" positively. We want to prove this with the book by the famous French anarchist Sebastian Faure, "My Communism: Universal Happiness", which appeared in 1921 and was published in Dutch by the "Roode Bibliotheek" in 1927.

Faure informs us of the purpose of his work as follows:

»This work describes the life of a great nation under libertarian communist rule in a simple, clear and attractive form and is intended to show that the anarchists have a richly studied social plan.«[39]

If we look at libertarian communism from the point of view of regulating production, it is not about creating equal economic conditions in which all producers control, administer and organize production *themselves*, not in the least.

Of course, we do not find an exact relationship between the producer and the entire social product, because the system works according to the motto "take as needed". However, this distribution system cannot be applied at the time of the takeover. In this phase, consumer goods are rationed according to a standard set for us by the masters of statistics. They "allocate" us how much we can use. Translated into a clear Marxist language, this means that the product is **not** available to the workers, and therefore

---

[39] Sebastian Faure, Het universele geluk, Roode Bibliotheek (My Communism: Universal Happiness) p. 5

they do not have the means of production. By the way, as we will see, Faure's libertarian communism leaves no doubt about this!

The regulation of operational life is understood here in the usual social democratic form, in which communism is only a question of technical organization.

While this summary of production in state communism is carried out by the authority of the state, in Faure it is created by »*the free and fraternal agreement*« (p. 6). But Faure is against any "authority". Therefore he says of these manifold connections in the life of the operation: »*This whole organization is based on the animating principle of free cooperation*« (p. 213 of the Dutch translation).

Here the phrase replaces the economic reality. We are still of the opinion that an economic system is based on *economic laws* and not on some kind of inspiring principle. This cannot be *the basis* for a production and reproduction process. If the producers want to have their rights secured, with or without the "animating principle", then the whole organization must be on a very material basis, then at least for the time being, the working time must be the *measure* for the share in social consumption. This seems quite clear to us.

c. The free agreement

For the mutual relationship of the producers, the relationships between the different operations, we find the same fluctuating, spongy ground again in the "free agreement".

Everything is very pleasant and cozy.

»People search, grope, summarize and try out the results of the various methods. The agreement appears, offers itself, pushes itself through its results and wins.« (S. 334)

Faure finds this basis of "freedom for all by agreement among all" very "natural". Because he says, isn't it the same in nature?

»Nature's example is there: clear and obvious. Everything is there connected by free and spontaneous agreement . . . The infinitely small things, a kind of dust, seek each other, attract each other, accumulate and form a core.« (p. 334).

We must note that examples borrowed from nature are always very dangerous, and it is precisely in this particular case that it, unfortunately, shows clearly and unambiguously how completely inadequate the libertarian method is. Everything is connected by free and spontaneous agreement. It is wonderful to see how thoughtlessly the human concept of "freedom" is transferred to nature, but metaphorically it is necessary.

But – Faure completely overlooks here the decisive moment of "free agreement" in nature. And that is that this "free agreement" is determined by the mutual forces of the allies. If the sun and the earth conclude the free agreement that the earth is to run around the sun in 365 1/4 days, then this is determined among other things by **the mass** that the sun and earth have. *On this basis, the "free" agreement is concluded.*

This is what nature is all about. Its atoms, or electrons, or whatever one takes, come in mutual connection. The nature of this connection is determined by the forces which the allies have at their disposal. And therefore, we would like to take the example from nature, but to show that there must be an exact relationship between producer and product and an *exact relationship* between the different products if the "free agreement" is to be concluded in society. This agreement is then transformed from a phrase into a reality.

d. Central state production

If we now come to the organizational summary of the operational life, in order to make the apparatus usable for the needs of the people, Faure sketches a picture, of which the Bolsheviks could be proud, because it is not different from the "General Cartel" of Hilferding!

The production will work for the demand, and

»it is, therefore, necessary above all to determine the total of the need and the quantity of each need.« (p. 215).

This is done by each municipality reporting needs by population to the "main administration office of the nation", where officials get an overview of the total needs of the whole population. Then each municipality publishes a second list with the indication of how much it can produce, whereby the "main administration" now knows the productive forces of the "nation".

The solution is very clear. The top officials should now determine what part of the production falls on each community, and *»what part of the production they can keep for themselves.«* (S. 216)

This course is exactly the same as the state communists imagine it to be. Below are the masses, above are the officials who manage production and distribution. Thus, society is not grounded in economic realities, but dependent on the good or bad will or the ability of certain persons; to remove any doubt regarding the central right of disposal, he adds:

»The main administration knows how large the total production and the total demand is and must, therefore, inform each

district committee how much product it can dispose of and how much means of production it must procure.« (S. 218).

Where the "libertarian-communist" part of the system now lies, we completely miss it. Perhaps our readers are smarter so that they can solve the mystery for us. To simplify this solution, let us once again reprint the social democratic position of Hilferding:

»... all decisions as to method, place, quantity, and available tools involved in the production of new goods are made by ... the local regional or national commissars of the socialist society. (With the) knowledge of the requirements of their society by means of comprehensively organized statistics of production and consumption ... they can thus shape, with conscious foresight, the whole economic life of the communities of which they are the appointed representatives and leaders in accordance with the needs of the members.«[40]

As long as our readers have not solved the mystery for us, we find that the **right of disposal** over the production apparatus is assigned to those who are familiar with the tricks of <u>statistics</u>. And perhaps we have learned so much from the political economy that it gives them *power* in society.

---

[40] Rudolf Hilferding, Finance Capital, Chapter 1, www.marxists.org/archive/hilferding/1910/finkap/

This "main administration" **must** obtain the means to assert itself, i.e., it **must create a state vis-à-vis the workers who are "animated" by another principle**,

who want to establish an exact relationship from producer to the product!

This is one of the laws of movement of this "libertarian" system, whether Faure means it or not.

Nor does it matter whether the dish is served with the sauce of "free agreements" or with the "soulful principle". This does not disturb the political and economic laws.

One cannot blame Faure for forging the whole economy into one. But this synthesis is a *development process* that the producers have to carry out *themselves* within the operations. Therefore, the first requirement is that there is a basis on which they can do this *themselves*, i.e., *the introduction of the working time account is the first requirement!*

Then no "main administration" has to assign anything anymore.

e. Anarcho-Syndicalism

In 1927 the "Gemengd Syndicalistisch Verbond" published a brochure by Müller Lehning with the title "Anarcho-Syndicalisme" to spread the principles of the anarcho-syndicalist trade union movement as it is organized in the *International Workers' Association* (IWA-headquarters Madrid).

First, the author unmistakably criticizes the anarchists, a critique that, in reality, means nothing more than: You are only phraseologists. The anarchists should, therefore, drop the phrases and become practical people, anarcho-syndicalists.

He opposes the well-known view that it is first a question of smashing everything to see later how things can be put right again (p. 4). What is necessary is a program *»how the realization of anarcho-syndicalism comes about after the revolution.«* (p. 5).

It is not enough just to propagate the economic revolution, *»but one must also examine how it must be carried out.«* (p. 6).

The anarchists in Russia put the self-initiative of the masses in the foreground, *»but what this initiative had to be, what the masses had to do, today and tomorrow, everything remained blurred and little positive.«* (p. 7).

»Many manifestos may have appeared, but few could give a clear and unambiguous answer to the question of daily practice.« (p. 8).

»We may say that the Russian Revolution once and forever asked the question:

What are the practical and economic foundations of a society without a wage system?

What to do the day after the revolution? Anarchism will have to answer this question; it will have to learn the lesson of these last years if total failure is not to end in irreversible bankruptcy.

The old anarchist slogans, *however much truth they contain and* **however often they are repeated, do not solve any of the problems posed by real life.** *In particular, they do not solve any of the problems posed by the social revolution of the working class.«* (p. 10)

And Müller Lehning continues:

»Without these practical realities, all propaganda remains negative, and all ideals remain utopias. This is the lesson anarchism has to learn from history, and it cannot be sufficiently repeated by the tragic development of the Russian revolution.« (p. 11)

And what alternative does anarchism syndicalism propose? What are the practical foundations for a society without a wage system?

Anarcho-syndicalism is just as stubbornly silent about this as anarchism. The author develops a kind of program for the construction of anarcho-syndicalist operational life, but it does not contain a single word about the *economic foundations*!

The problem is once again considered from a social-democratic point of view: from the point of view of the *organizational* consolidation of operational life.

The Russian Revolution, in particular, has shown that the problem is not this: How do we build the operational life, whether federal or central, but the question is: Which *economic* conditions is the operational life subject to so that the workers can control and lead the production **themselves**?

Müller Lehning then develops an organizational program:

»*The economic organizations have the goal of expropriating the state and capitalism. The organs of state and capitalism must be replaced by the productive associations of the workers, as carriers of the whole economic life. The basis must be the operation; the operating organization must form the nucleus for the new economic social organization. The whole system of production must be built on the federation of industry and agriculture.*« (p.18)

It should be noted that this refers to the construction of the anarcho-syndicalist trade union movement. Workers must organize themselves into industrial and agricultural federations so that **their** organizations can take over operational life after the revolution. The transport company would then be run by the transport association, the mines by the miners' association, and so on.

In other words, the anarcho-syndicalist trade union movement sees itself as the future carrier of economic life.

From this point of view, there can only be a proletarian revolution if the anarcho-syndicalist trade union movement is strong enough to run the factory life.

This is why Muller Lehning writes:

»The purpose of economic organizations is to expropriate the state and capitalism.«

Thus, the organizational extent of the anarcho-syndicalist trade union movement becomes the **yardstick** by which "maturity" for social revolution is determined.

In the northern countries of Europe, where anarcho-syndicalism has no organizational significance, the workers who represent this movement feel very well that their organization cannot be a yardstick for revolution and therefore reject this consequence. But because they have no idea of the *economic* foundations of the communist economy, they have no ground under their feet and can do nothing but rely on the organizational control of the revolution by the trade union movement.

The anarcho-syndicalist trade union movement can, therefore, best be investigated where it actually matters. And that is in Spain.

Of course, it cannot be our intention here to subject the anarcho-syndicalist trade union movement in Spain, the C.N.T., to general criticism. At this point, we are only interested in what considerations prevail here concerning the implementation of the communist economy. And there does not seem to be the slightest doubt that the C.N.T., *as a trade union*, demands the management and administration of economic life for itself.

This can be seen, for example, from the fact that it demands:

»*...the union's control over production.*« ("De Syndicalist", 19 September 1931)

and not the control of the broad masses by their councils.

Even the course of the C.N.T. Congress in June 1931 leaves no room for doubt in this respect. In the French syndicalist magazine "La Revolution Proletarienne" of July 1931 there is a report about this congress, from which we take:

»*The Congress shows that the C.N.T. is an enormous force. The only thing that remains is to specify and put into practice its measures for the takeover of the industry.*«

You can see that the C.N.T. must carry out the seizure. That's why Müller Lehning wrote:

»The economic organizations have as their goal the expropriation of the state and capitalism.«

And the French report on the C.N.T. Congress also states:

»The Congress has decided to demand the expropriation of all domains over 50 hectares by handing over land, livestock, and equipment to the farmworkers' unions.«

And to clear up misunderstandings about the socialization plans of the anarcho-syndicalist trade union movement, the "Syndicalist" reported on August 29, 1931:

»There are several militants in the National Committee of the C.N.T. who do not believe that the C.N.T. in its present condition is ready to <u>take over production</u>.«

What a misunderstanding about the fundamental problems of the social revolution!

Why does anarcho-syndicalism refuse to cast a glance under the mysterious veil that lies over the traffic of products between operations in the communist economy?

On what economic bases does consumption take place?

What is the economic basis of the producer in relation to the social wealth of goods?

We hear nothing about it! That is a bad sign. For that means nothing other than referring here to the "economic" foundations of the libertarian communism of the French anarchist Faure. There is no other way. Therefore, as an economic critique of anarcho-syndicalism, we are applying exactly what we have already written about Faure. The economic critique of Faure's libertarian communism is also the critique of anarcho-syndicalism.

6.
The social production process in general

a. Production and reproduction

Through its production apparatus, humanity has created an organ to meet its diverse needs. With the help of machines and tools, human labor fights against nature in order to distribute a stream of labor products over the earth using natural raw materials. This working process is the *production process*. It not only produces goods but also absorbs many machines and tools as well as the labor itself. From this point of view, the production process is a process of *demolition*, of *destruction*. But at the same time, we create new values in this process of destruction: machines, tools, and our labor are consumed, but at the same time, renewed, restored, **re**produced. The social production process runs like the life process in the human body: through self-destruction to self-construction in a continuously more complicated form.

»Whatever the form of the process of production in a society, it must be a continuous process, must continue to go periodically through the same phases ... When viewed, therefore, as a connected whole, and as flowing on with incessant renewal,

every social process of production is, at the same time, a process of reproduction.«[41]

b. Capitalist production

It is precisely in the laws of movement of this constant renewal, in the laws of movement of reproduction, that capitalism presents itself as an uncontrolled and revolutionary system. It knows no standstill. It is constantly pulled from its old foundations to find a new balance at a higher level, with a higher capacity. It *must* create more and more and bigger companies, it must reproduce production on an ever-larger scale, or to put it capitalistically: Capital <u>must</u> *accumulate* constantly.

Because the profitability of capital is the purpose of capitalist production, and therefore *profit* is the driving power. And because only the living labor power can generate *surplus value*, every capitalist must strive to employ as many workers as possible, that is, to produce as much as possible.

In this quest for profit, the various business groups face each other. Each group wants to secure as much as possible of the surplus-value that is squeezed out of the working class. The hunt for the

---

[41] Karl Marx, Capital Volume 1, p. 401

prey becomes a *mutual battle for the prey*, or to put it simply, they compete against each other.

This fight for prey is the great revolutionary in production. Every company has to be prepared to produce cheaper than its competitors so that the pursuit of profit means the pursuit of technical improvements and ever newer, labor-saving machines have to replace the old ones. If a company, for example, in the steel industry, succeeds in finding a new, cheaper production method, this company will have reduced the value of the capital of all its competitors. The other capitals are obsolete, or, as Marx calls it, the victim of "moral wear and tear". However, this only means that the profitability base of these capitals has disappeared, so new capital must be added if the old capital is not to be completely destroyed.

It goes beyond the scope of our considerations to address the immense waste of social goods, as well as the crisis and other disasters that the struggle for prey entails. For our subject, it is only important to point out that the constant renewal, the *reproduction* of the tools, is *an individual function of the capitalists*. It is up to them to decide *whether and to what extent* it will be renewed, not, of course, by taking the needs of the people as a guide, but by concentrating on the profit opportunities offered by the struggle for prey at this moment.

7.
The communist production

a. The transfer of the goods

Before we take a closer look at the general rules of production and distribution, for a good understanding, we must first understand why communism has no **exchange** and no **value**. We have seen that the explanation of the official text interpreters regarding the Hilferding`s "General Cartel" in the Marxist sense cannot be correct. So, the question rightly arises: If it is *not* so, then *what* is it like?

Despite all the learned books written on this subject, the abolition of these categories is still hidden in the deepest darkness. But it is especially important not to make things more difficult than they really are. The point is that you have *to own* something in order to exchange it. Those who have nothing, who own nothing, have nothing to trade. The exchange is, therefore, not only an economic act but rather a transfer *based on private property*. Exchange is, therefore, an economic act that expresses *the social relationship* that the products of labor are privately owned. The social revolution, the revolution in social relations, the revolution in the mutual relations of people in the social life of operational units, abolishes this *social relationship*: it brings the products of labor into common ownership. Exchange, which is a function of private property, is thus abolished,

»... *because under the altered circumstances no one can give anything except his labor, and because, on the other hand, nothing can pass to the ownership of individuals, except individual means of consumption.*«[42]

In communism, operational units are equal parts of a closed whole, of the entire production and distribution process. Each operational unit carries out only one partial activity by passing on its product to the other until it is suitable for consumption.

However, this transfer of goods is not an "*exchange*", because the "owners" of the products do not change in the flow of goods. The *new legal relationship* between the producer and the manufactured product is, therefore, the same as for the means of production: it *belongs to the community*. Just as operational units receive machines, buildings, and raw materials to process them *independently* for the community according to certain rules, they must also *independently pass on* their products according to the rules applicable in the production process or consumption. The

---

[42] Karl Marx, Critique of the Gotha Programme, www.marxists.org/archive/marx/works/download/Marx_Critque_of_the_Gotha_Programme.pdf

operational units thus direct and control the production **and** distribution of their products "in the name of society", i.e., in responsibility *to* society.

Common parlance, however, does not distinguish so exactly between economic terms. In ordinary language, therefore, attention is paid only to the nature of the transfer of goods, which, of course, also takes place constantly in communism. And here, this transfer is perhaps also called **exchange**, even if this transfer has meanwhile assumed a completely different content. However, we do not want to set a bad example by using an old word for a new term, and that is why we are constantly talking about the *transfer* of goods.

b. The production time

The same conceptual transformation takes place in relation to the **value**. The exchange of goods does not take place arbitrarily but in a certain proportion. The exchange takes place on the basis that the goods embody the *same* amount of social work. This amount of labor is its value. The value is, therefore, the socially necessary amount of work that is in a product.

It is immediately noticeable, however, that it is precisely a demand of the communist economy that we need »to know how much labor each article of consumption requires for its production«.[43] (Engels)

It follows, then, that transfer of goods in capitalism comes about on the basis of the social work contained in the products – and also in communism! Just as the transfer of goods in capitalism comes about on the basis of value, so it also *seems* to be in communism.

But this is by no means the case. The contradiction of capitalist production is: *social production,* on the one hand, *private property* on the other.

The movement of goods takes place because of private owners "*exchange*" **their** goods.

The relationship in which the goods are exchanged is determined by their *value*, i.e., by the socially necessary labor needed for their production. However, through the private ownership of the means of production, social labor itself, as labor power, also becomes a commodity - i.e., it is exchanged by the wage laborers on the same basis as the commodities.

In the goods movement of capitalism, the antagonism of capitalist production is thus expressed once

---

[43] Frederick Engels, Anti-Dühring, Part III: Socialism, IV. Distribution https://www.marxists.org/archive/marx/works/1877/anti-duhring/

again: Exchange of values - i.e., social work as private property.

In communism, the separation between producers and means of production was abolished. The means of production are no longer the property of a separate class; social production is administered collectively.

The products are not *transferred* by private owners but *transferred* within the community. The goods are transported based on the working time required by society.

In communism, the contradiction between social production and private property is abolished.

In the movement of goods under communism - the distribution of goods - the unity of common management and social production is expressed.

From this, we can see that in communist operational life, the amount of work required for the production of individual objects of daily use means something quite different than "value". And now it is quite possible again that in common usage, the "value" of goods in communism is spoken of, although the term has acquired a completely different meaning. Here, too, we do not want to set a bad example by using an old word for a new term, so that we speak of the **production time** of the goods.

Instead of saying that the flow of goods through *exchange* moves on the basis of *value*, we, therefore, say that the flow of goods is *transferred on the basis of production time*. Although the movement is externally the same as in capitalism, the form of movement has been completely changed by the elimination of the value-form of money and the *content* of the term through the transition to common ownership. Or as Marx puts it:

»Within the c o - o p e r a t i v e (highlighting GIC) society based on common ownership of the means of production, the producers do not exchange their products; just as little does the labor employed on the products appear here as the **value** *of these products, as a material quality possessed by them, since now, in contrast to capitalist society, individual labor no longer exists in an indirect fashion (the detour of private property - GIC) but directly as a component part of total labor.«*[44]

»Here, obviously, the same principle prevails as that which regulates the exchange of commodities, as far as this is exchange of equal values. Content and form are changed, because under the altered circumstances no one can give anything except his labor, and because, on the other hand, nothing can

---

[44] Karl Marx, Critique of the Gotha Programme, www.marxists.org/archive/marx/works/download/Marx_Critque_of_the_Gotha_Programme.pdf

pass to the ownership of individuals, except individual means of consumption.«[45]

From this we can see that communism by Marx is by no means a "negative system". Instead of the regulating functions of money, there is the registration of the flow of goods, the social accounting, based on the average social working time and thus based on the average social production time, which is carried out in the *cooperative context* of producers and consumers. The market, which is a measure of needs for capitalists, is completely abolished - it is abolished by the direct connection between consumer organizations and production.

This connection is the very subject of *planned production*. Although the socialist economists go beyond their fantasies in this very area, in a later consideration of the "market", the planned production is treated only marginally by us. The reason for this is that it does not fall within the scope of this writing: it falls outside the *fundamental principles* of operational life. The planned production can only be built based on economic principles. Therefore, these principles must first be clarified. The planned production is, therefore, a completely different subject, but since the experiences of the Russian Revolution, it can also fall into the area of exact research. (See also:

---

[45] Karl Marx, Critique of the Gotha Programme

Friedrich Pollock, The Planned Economy Trials in the Soviet Union 1917–1927. This work does not provide any criticism of Russia but only wants to show how the struggle for market control has taken place over the last ten years and is still taking place.

c. The method of investigation

To further investigate the *transfer* of goods based on *production time*, we use the usual method of simplification. For this reason, we will not at this stage consider any complications that might result from a change in the average social production time, such as the improvement of the rationality of operation and technological progress, in order to investigate the effects of these factors step by step. For the time being, we assume a simple reproduction, i.e., we assume that society does *not* decide to expand the production apparatus in order to dedicate a later chapter to the functioning of production on an expanded basis.

d. Communist reproduction

After these preliminary remarks, we can present the course of the communist economic life in a very simple and clear form. Each company calculates how much working time is spent on its product, i.e., it determines how many working hours of "fixed" means of production (machines and buildings), how many working hours of "circulating" means of production (raw materials and consumables) and how many directly consumed working hours flow into the product. Regardless of the type of operation, whether it is a sugar factory, a railway company or an administrative body, it always consumes inputs, raw materials and consumables, and direct work performed, so that each operation can determine the number of working hours that the product passes on to society. Or to put it another way:

Each operation works according to the *production equation*:

f + c + l = product

(machinery and buildings) + (raw materials, consumables) + (labor) = product

Note: Transport companies and administrative bodies do not provide a "product" but a "service". But that doesn't change anything: we'll come back to that later.

If, for the sake of clarity, we replace the letters with fictitious numbers, the production, for example in a shoe factory, would be shown in the following scheme:

(f + c) + l = product

1,250 working hours + 61,250 working hours + 62,500 working hours = 125,000 working hours

machines etc. + raw materials + work = 40,000 pairs of shoes

That's an average of 3.125 hours per pair.

However, if the shoe company wants to start a new production period, it has to replenish everything that has been lost in production. It must restore its wear and tear on production equipment (1,250 hours), re-purchase raw materials (61,250 hours) and reinstate 62,500 working hours of workers. After that, production can start again in the *same* way. The production equation thus immediately proves to be a *reproduction formula*.

Each company reproduces itself. And thus, the entire social-economic life is reproduced.

To give the entire economy a clear form, we use the same production equation as we did for each individual company. In this formula, we find *all* the means of production available to society, as well as *all* the raw and auxiliary materials and *all* the working hours used by the workers directly in production. The entire economic life is thus represented:

$(F_t + C_t) + L_t =$ Total product

Note: The $_t$ index means: total.

If for accuracy reasons, we use fictitious numbers for this purpose, we get, for example:

$F_t + C_t + L_t$ = Total product

108 million + 650 million + 650 million = 1,408 million working hours

The product mass of the entire social product thus comprises 1,408 million working hours. All operations together now take 108 million working hours of production materials from this mass, a further 650 million of raw materials and consumables. At the same time, the rest or 650 million is accounted for by the individual consumption of the workers. This means that the entire social product is consumed, while *all* operations are reproduced so that a new production period can begin.

e. Reproduction of labor power

Nevertheless, it is necessary to consider individual consumption for a moment. It is true that in our example, there are 650 million available for this purpose, but that does not say how the product is distributed among the workers!

For example, unskilled, learned and intellectual work may be *evaluated* differently. The distribution could be, for example, that the unskilled person is paid 3/4 hours for an hour worked, the learned person just one hour, the civil servant 1 1/2 hours, and the manager 3 hours. A 40-hour week is recorded in the company books: 30 hours for unskilled workers, 40 hours for skilled workers, 60 hours for civil servants, and 120 hours for managers.

In fact, economists take this view. It does not occur to them to "value" the work equally, i.e., to give everyone the same share of the social product. That is the meaning of Neurath's **"life circumstances"**. (See chapter 2d).

The "nutrition physiologists" will determine a subsistence minimum that the "income" of the unskilled represents, while the others receive more according to the ratio of their diligence, their abilities, and the importance of their work.

Kautsky considers this difference in "remuneration" to be "necessary" because he believes that »*higher wages should be paid for unpleasant or heavy work than for pleasant and light work.*«[46]

He also believes that this is a reason why the calculation of working hours is not practicable. With his colleague Leichter, he goes so far as to maintain the wage difference even within a profession because

---

[46] K. Kautsky, The proletarian revolution and its program, p. 318

the individual wages would have to rise with the routine of the skilled worker over the basic wage. This also informs their position on the retention of piece work in communism. Leichter, on the other hand, rightly notes that this is not an obstacle to the calculation of working hours, as we can see from our example. He says:

»*All that remains is the purely technical difficulty, also present in capitalism, of setting the wages for the individual jobs, but that does not mean any complication in comparison with the capitalist method.*«[47]

So, we note that of this kind of communists, the different payment of the different kinds of work, even of the individual differences within the same kind of work, is, in principle, considered right. But this means nothing other than that even in communism the "*struggle for better working conditions*" does not stop, that the distribution of the social product of production has an antagonistic character and *that the struggle for the distribution of the product is continued*. This struggle is and will be a struggle for power.

Surely it cannot be demonstrated more clearly than that these gentlemen cannot imagine a society in which the working class is not dominated. For them, people have simply become *objects*. People are nothing

---

[47] Otto Leichter, Die Wirtschaftsrechnung in der sozialistischen Gesellschaft, p. 76

more than parts of the production apparatus, for which nutrition physiologists have to calculate how much food has to be supplied to this material (subsistence minimum) to have new labor power available. The working class must fight with the greatest energy against such a view and demand the same share of social wealth for all.

f. The Value of Labor Power in Life-Circumstances Communism

The reason why the "communist" economists cannot get rid of the difference in the valuation of labor is, we think, their class feeling. An equal distribution of the social product completely contradicts this powerful bastion of conceptualization and therefore seems "impossible" to them. However, if not an old principle, it is certainly a correct one that the world of thought is mainly guided by the world of emotions, and that the mind will not find much else than that which corresponds to the world of emotions. From this, it can be explained that, e.g., Leichter wants to abolish the concept of value for objective production but cannot free himself from it concerning the labor power. The difference in the appreciation of the different types of labor power in capitalism is because the labor power is a "commodity" that can be bought just like other "commodities. The average price the entrepreneur pays for it is as high as it is necessary to reproduce the labor power. For the unskilled worker, the value is as high as the food cost for the lowest "existence minimum". The children of the unskilled generally cannot learn a profession because they have to earn as much as possible immediately. Thus, the unskilled have <u>themselves</u> reproduced the unskilled labor power again.

More is needed to reproduce the skilled labor. Here the children learn a profession, and thus the learned have reproduced the learned labor power themselves. The same applies to intellectuals. For Leichter, this "commodity character of the labor power also applies to "socialism". He says:

»Differently qualified workers (port workers, civil servants, engineers - GIC) need a different amount of effort to reproduce their labor power. Qualified workers need more to reproduce their labor power for the next day for the next year, i.e., their current expenses are greater. However, more effort is needed to rebuild a qualified labor power as a whole, i.e., a person with the same level of education and knowledge, if the former carrier of this labor power is no longer able to work. All this must be included in the various assessments of the labor power.«[48]

---

[48] Otto Leichter, Die Wirtschaftsrechnung in der sozialistischen Gesellschaft (The economic account in the socialist community), p. 61

g. The value of labor in capitalism according to Marx

If we look here at the Marxist analysis of the value of the labor power, it is perfectly clear that the *wage laws* for capitalism and life-circumstances communism are completely identical! Marx says:[49]

»What, then, is the cost of production of labor-power? It is the cost required for the maintenance of the laborer as a laborer, and for his education and training as a laborer. Therefore, the shorter the time required for training up to a particular sort of work, the smaller is the cost of production of the worker, the lower is the price of his labor-power, his wages. In those branches of industry in which hardly any period of apprenticeship is necessary, and the mere bodily existence of the worker is sufficient, the cost of his production is limited almost exclusively to the commodities necessary for keeping him in working condition.

The price of his work will therefore be determined by the price of the necessary means of subsistence.

Here, however, there enters another consideration. The manufacturer who calculates his cost of production and, in accordance with it, the price of the product, takes into account the

---

[49] Marx assumes here that the price corresponds to the value, i.e. that there is a balance between supply and demand on the labor market.

wear and tear of the instruments of labor. If a machine costs him, for example, 1,000 shillings, and this machine is used up in 10 years, he adds 100 shillings annually to the price of the commodities, in order to be able after 10 years to replace the worn-out machine with a new one. In the same manner, the cost of production of simple labor-power must i n c l u d e t h e c o s t o f p r o p a g a t i o n , by means of which the race of workers is enabled to multiply itself, and to replace worn-out workers with new ones. The wear and tear of the worker, therefore, is calculated in the same manner as the wear and tear of the machine. Thus, the cost of production of simple labor-power amounts to the cost of the existence and propagation of the worker. The price of this cost of existence and propagation constitutes wages. The wages thus determined are called the m i n i m u m o f w a g e s .«[50]

Just as the reproduction of the "objective" part of the production apparatus is an *individual function of the capitalist*, so the reproduction of the labor power is an *individual function of the worker*. But just as the reproduction of the objective part of the production apparatus becomes a social function in communism, so also the reproduction of the labor power becomes a social function. It is no longer im-

---

[50] Karl Marx, Wage Labor and Capital, p. 12, https://www.marxists.org/archive/marx/works/download/pdf/wage-labour-capital.pdf

posed on different individuals, but carried by society. Teaching is no longer tied to Papa's wallet but depends solely on the child's disposition and physical condition. It cannot be the idea of communism to give individuals, who are endowed by nature with more favorable hereditary factors or more favorable abilities and thus have the possibility to enjoy to the fullest extent all achievements of human society in the field of culture, art and science, on top of that even a larger share of the social product than those that are less fortunate physically or psychologically by nature.

But there is more.

The distribution of the social product in communism is not a simple reproduction of labor power: it is the distribution of all material and intellectual riches that humanity produces with its technology and thus goes far beyond the simple reproduction of the labor power. What "communists" à la Kautsky, Leichter, Neurath want with their "life circumstances" amounts to ensuring the "lower" worker a "subsistence minimum" based on nutrition physiology, while the "higher" consume abundance. That is to say:

In reality, they do not think of abolishing exploitation. Based on the common possession of means of production, the exploitation is continued!

In the "life circumstances communism," the producers give their labor power to a great, indefinable "*something*" which is euphemistically called "society". But where this "*something*" appears, it is an element alien to the producers that rises above them, exploits them and rules over them, as "something" that is the actual ruler of the production apparatus, as a "community" in which they are included as "objects", as production factors.

8.
The socially average working hour as the basis of production!

a. Kautskyan problems

We have previously pointed out (see Chapter 4c) that Max Weber and Ludwig Mises were able to reap their laurels by defeating the working time calculation, and how Kautsky proved to be a very clever student. In his book: »The proletarian revolution and its program«[51], he gives proof of this. But with that, he comes to the difficulty that he must now turn against Marx. In his usual loyalty he does not, of course, do this, but declares the calculation of working hours theoretically conceivable, but unsuitable for practical implementation. Before he begins to explain these considerations, he first gives a formulation of the working time calculation. Still, it should be noted that he accidentally forgets to mention that this was Marx's point of view.

Kautsky first shows the impossibility of production without a unit of account and concludes that

---

[51] *Die proletarische Revolution und ihr Programm*, Dietz, Stuttgart, 2nd edition 1922, https://archive.org/details/dieproletarische00kaut/

»The continuity of money is indispensable as a measure of value for accounting and the calculation of exchange ratios in a socialist society.«[52]

But then he asks:

»But will it require the same money that still exists today, or that should exist, after all, the money that is formed from a special commodity, usually gold? Instead of this product and representatives of human labor, could one not directly define human labor itself as a measure of value and create labor money that directly certifies work done? This would be conceivable, for example, in the form that every worker receives a certificate for every working hour he has completed; for this certificate, he receives the right to the product of one working hour. For each product, the amount of work it cost would have to be calculated in this way. For the wage of one working day, the worker could always buy products whose manufacture took one working day. The calculation would always have to be correct, any exploitation would be impossible, and the worker would have complete freedom in how he wanted to invest his wages. Any paternalism by an authority that allocates rations to the individual would be avoided.

---

[52] Karl Kautsky, Die proletarische Revolution und ihr Programm (The proletarian revolution and its program), p. 318

There is no doubt that such kind of money would be conceivable. But could it also be done in practice?«[53]

Oh, no! Too bad it's not possible! And why is that not possible? Because Kautsky believes that the difference in wages and the piecework prevents this and because he still regards communism as the monster cartel of Hilferding, in which the production managers control the entire economy from their central government offices! In this way, he reaches a completely wrong conclusion. His question has the following character:

With the abolition of private property, the entire social-economic life is united into one unit. The products move from one company to another until the "end product" is suitable for consumption. The whole world is involved in the transfer of semi-finished products and raw materials: Thousands and thousands of workers provided their labor power before, for example, a pair of shoes was ready for consumption, before they appeared as "finished products". *But how many working hours does this end product contain?*

That's the formulation of Kautsky's riddle, and he desperately lets his head sink in such an inhuman

---

[53] Karl Kautsky, Die proletarische Revolution und ihr Programm (The proletarian revolution and its program), p. 318. Highlighting by GIK

task. Yes. Theoretically, of course, the solution must be possible. But practical? No, it is impossible

»to calculate for each product the amount of work it has cost from its first beginnings until its completion, including transport and other ancillary works.«[54] »...the estimation of the goods according to work contained in them, (even) the most tremendous and perfect statistical apparatus cannot ... achieve.«[55]

Indeed, Kautsky is absolutely right that in this way, it is impossible. However, such a method of production calculation exists only in Kautsky's imagination.

b. Leichter's answer

Even if Leichter fully agrees with Kautsky that a society without exploitation belongs to the fantasies of the Millennial Kingdom, he knows much better than his grey party colleague how the calculations in production work. He emphasizes that within a trust or cartel, goods are never transferred without "settlement" and that this will also be the case in communism.

---

[54] Karl Kautsky, Die proletarische Revolution und ihr Programm (The proletarian revolution and its program), p. 318
[55] As above p. 321

»... there are relations between the individual production sites, and this relationship will continue to exist in the world as long as there is a division of labor, and the division of labor in this higher sense will continue to develop with the progress of technology.«[56]

»All material conditions of production, all semi-finished materials, all raw materials, all auxiliary materials, which are delivered from other production sites to the processing plant, will be debited, invoiced to it.«[57]

»The cartel magnates or - in a socialist economy - the leaders of the entire economy, will not have different companies produced with the same program according to different methods and with different costs. This is also often an incentive for weak entrepreneurs to let themselves be "swallowed" by a giant corporation in capitalism nolens volens since they hope that now also for "their" business the most appropriate organization within the cartel, the best manufacturing method, the most capable office employees will be used to increase the productivity of their business.

For this, however, it is necessary to record the results of all operations separately and to do so - no matter whether in capitalist or socialist economy - as if each operation had

---

[56] Otto Leichter, Die Wirtschaftsrechnung in der sozialistischen Gesellschaft (The economic account in the socialist community), p. 54
[57] As above p. 68

its own entrepreneur who wants to become clear about the economic result of production. Therefore, there is very strict accounting within the cartel, and it belongs to the amateurish idea of capitalism and also of socialism if one thinks that within the cartel goods can be moved without further accounting, in short, that the individual group operations do not know very well how to differentiate between **"mine and yours.**«[58]

There is thus a "settlement" between the different operations. Even within each individual operation, the books are kept according to the latest and most accurate methods. For reasons that cannot be examined here in more detail, capitalist management was forced to switch to rationalization around 1921, and around 1922 a completely new literature was produced, which developed the methods of calculating the exact cost price for each individual method, for each individual partial work. This is composed of many factors, as: Consumption of means of production, raw and auxiliary materials, a certain standard for social insurance, as well as for the office staff, etc. General formulas can, therefore, be used to calculate the "production costs" for each individual item.

---

[58] Otto Leichter, The economic account in the socialist community), p. 52f. Highlighting by GIK

Leichter explains:

»*Capitalist accounting, when carried out perfectly and smoothly in a factory, can at any time accurately determine the value of a semi-finished product, a piece of work in production, the costs of each individual operation. It can determine in which of several workshops of a factory, on which of several machines, with which of several workers a work ration is cheaper, it can thus, at any time, increase the rationality of the production process to the highest level. Besides, there is another achievement of the capitalist accounting method; in every large factory, there are several expenses and expenditures that are not directly included in the exchangeable end product. (This refers to salaries of office employees, heating of localities, etc. GIC) ... It is also one of the great achievements of the capitalist accounting method to have made possible these subtleties in the economic accounts.*«[59]

However, the formulas as they are currently used in a certain enterprise are not suitable in communism, because various factors that are now included in the cost accounting, such as interest on capital, do not apply to us and because they are based on the common denominator of *money*. Still, *the method, as such, is a lasting advance*. Also, in this respect, the new society is born from the womb of the old one.

---

[59] Otto Leichter, Die Wirtschaftsrechnung in der sozialistischen Gesellschaft (The economic account in the socialist community), p. 22f

c. The progress

From this point of view, the impossible calculation of the work involved in a product appears in a completely different light. What Kautsky cannot do from his economic center, *the producers themselves can do very well*. The secret is that every operational unit, managed and administered by its operational organization, acts as an "independent" unit, just as in capitalism.

»At first sight, one might think that each individual production plant is quite independent. Still, if one looks closer, one will clearly see the umbilical cord through which the individual plant is connected with the rest of the economy and its management.«[60]

Each "independent" unit has an "end product," and by applying the formula $(f+c)+l$, it can calculate at any time how much work is necessary for its product. Finally, when the "final plant" has finished its "final product" so that it can be consumed, we know immediately how much work it has involved "from the beginning to the final product, including transport and other ancillary activities". Just as production is made up of sub-processes, the calculation of working time is also made up, a calculation that

---

[60] Otto Leichter, Die Wirtschaftsrechnung in der sozialistischen Gesellschaft (The economic account in the socialist community), p. 100f

is entirely in the hands of the producers and is therefore not a function of Kautsky's economic headquarters.

Kautsky, therefore, recognizes the need to calculate the average social working time of the products, but he does not see any possibility of putting this concept into concrete terms. So it's no wonder that he can't get anywhere at all with the problems around this point. For example, he is already stuck in the diversity of productivity of the operations, in the question of the progress of technology and in the "price" of the products.

Although it may be superfluous, after we have uncovered his fundamental mistakes, to deal even more closely with his objections, we want to follow up his observations for the concrete version of the category of socially average working time.

d. The difference in company productivity

For this purpose, we initially concentrate on the "prices" of the products. He points out that not all companies are equally productive. One company has a better location than another, or it has a better organization of production, or there are better machines: in short, the production costs differ slightly in all companies that produce the same product, perhaps even significantly. For example, one shoe factory can produce shoes in 3.125 hours, another in 3 1/2 hours, and another in 3 hours per pair. Thus, each company gets a different production time, and each company has its own *operational average*.

The social production, however, is about determining the *social average*, i.e., how much work is invested in a pair of shoes, calculated over the entire social shoe production. It is, therefore, no different from the average of all shoe factories in the district. For example, in the examples we mentioned, it would be possible for the *social average* to be 3,3 hours per pair.

It is, therefore, a remarkable fact. In our example, the social average could be 3,3 hours per pair, while no operation works according to this average! There is a contradiction between the actual labor input in each individual operation, the average of the operation, and the social average.

This contradiction will *always* exist, even if the communist economic life is perfectly organized. Because two operational units will rarely be completely the same, technological progress alone means that there will always be differences, because if a new type of machine is introduced, it will not be put into operation simultaneously everywhere.

It is this contradiction that confronts Kautsky with insurmountable difficulties and leads him to claim the "impossibility" of calculating working hours. He asks:

»And what work should be charged? Certainly not the one that actually each individual product cost. The different copies of the same type would have different prices, those produced under less favorable conditions higher than the others. But that would be absurd. They would all have to have the same price, and that would have to be calculated, not according to work really spent, but according to the socially necessary work.«[61]

Kautsky rightly demands here that the "prices" of the products (we will use its terminology for a moment) must correspond to the socially necessary work. This is *not* the work that was actually spent on the product in each individual operational unit because the time actually spent is sometimes above and sometimes below the average.

The solution to the problem, however, is once again that the producers *themselves*, i.e., their *accounting* department, calculate this social average and not Kautsky! What the leaders of Hilferding`s "General Cartel" cannot do, *the producers themselves can do very well!*

---

[61] Karl Kautsky, Die proletarische Revolution und ihr Programm (The proletarian revolution and its program), p. 319. Highlighting by GIC

So, what is it all about?

It is a matter of determining the average of the entire footwear industry. We can see from this that the demand to determine the socially necessary work leads directly to an *accounting link* between similar operational units, the horizontal consolidation. In the very first transitional period, it will not go far beyond this accounting consolidation, but over time the accounting results must lead to mutual technical interpenetration. However, this horizontal merger is not a formation of a "cartel" carried out by the civil service and in which the producers are excluded from the control of the production process, but the merger grows *out of the operational units* themselves. The *"how"* and *"why"* is completely clear for every worker, "transparent", because firstly, the workers understand very well that they cannot "compete" against each other, and secondly, they soon learn that *planned production* is only possible based on the social average.

The connection of the individual operational units to *industrial branches* appears to be, therefore, similar to capitalist "cartel formation". Capitalist enterprises, however, join forces to maximize profits: They set prices in such a way that the *worst* company can still make a profit, giving the well-equipped factories additional profit. However, the communist industrial sector determines the average of all operational units.

Together the operational units have socially average productivity.

Precisely *because* the social average is calculated from all these operational units, the under- and over-productivities must balance each other out. The downward and upward deviations are therefore always zero. If all operational units, both under- and over-productive, pass on their products to society according to the *social* production time, the bookkeeping of the industrial sector must *always* be "balanced".

The elimination of the contradiction between the actual work carried out in each individual operational unit, and the social average is, therefore, a matter which is resolved *within* the sector. It is a question of accounting. *How* these accounts are kept does not fall within the framework of general theoretical considerations since this processing varies according to the type of operational unit. There are many ways of achieving this.

In principle, however, it is the following:

Footwear sector

Plant No. 1 produces 40,000 pairs of shoes in 3.125 hours, which is 125,000 hours.

Plant No. 2 produces 65,000 pairs of shoes in 3.5 hours, which is 227,500 hours.

Plant No. 3 produces 100,000 pairs of shoes in 3 hours, which is 300,000 hours.

The entire industry produces 205,000 pairs of shoes in 652,500 hours.

That is per pair: 652,500 / 205,000 equals 3.18 hours.

The operational averages are 3.125, 3.5, and 3 hours. The social average is 3.18 hours. Plant No. 1 has a production time that is below the social average and thus shows above-average productivity. Company No. 3, as well. Plant No. 2 works more time-consuming than the social average and is therefore below average productive. If the shoes are charged with 3.18 hours in consumption, then the operational units 1 and 3 have hours "over" in the accounting, which correspond to the "deficit" in the accounts of unit 2.

e. The progress of technology

But Kautsky has even more arrows in his quiver to prove the "impossibility" of the working time calculation. After showing what a "gigantic work" it would be to calculate the amount of work from start to finish, he says:

»And if you were finished, you would have to start all over again, since the technical conditions in some industries have changed in the meantime.«[62]

Yes, it's sad! After Kautsky has closely observed all sub-processes from his high vantage point, where the wires of production converge, he calculates how much working time is finally contained in the social end product. That is then "thank God" ready! But then the devilish technology comes and throws all his calculations over the top again!

But we have to hurry to calm Kautsky down. The amount of work the product needs after it has gone through all the sub-processes does not suddenly appear under the convulsive writing of his pencil, but the producers determine the working time for each sub-process. As technology advances or other productivity increases, the socially average working time *for this sub-process* decreases. If the product in question is coincidentally the end product for individual consumption, then it is transferred to consumption with a reduced average, and that is the

---

[62] Karl Kautsky, Die proletarische Revolution und ihr Programm (The proletarian revolution and its program) , p. 318f

end. However, if it is to be *transferred* to another company as f or c (as a means of production or as a raw material), the "costs" for this other operational unit are reduced so that it can also work "cheaper". In this way, the shortening of the social production time in a sector spreads to the entire economy without disturbing the calculations of others.

Kautsky's objections to the working time calculation all result from his crazy view of social production. He is stuck in the "General Cartel" and therefore speaks of "socially necessary work", but sees no possibility to give this term a concrete form. This is no wonder. It only takes on its concrete form through the management and administration of production in the hands of the producers by the "Association of free and equal producers".

From the practice of the revolutionary class struggle, which created the council system, the concrete version of the socially necessary working time was born at the same time.

9.
The social average working hour as the basis for consumption

a. Consumption as a function of production

Although the labor movement has already done very little to study the laws of movement of communist production, a much greater fog hangs over the relationship of producers to social consumer goods. This is not surprising, however. It was precisely the great progress in understanding the interrelationships of economic life that Marx illustrated how production, distribution, and consumption are not independent of each other but that they determine their forms mutually. It, therefore, seemed "superfluous", "utopian", and thus "unscientific" to take a closer look at the subject of communist consumption.

The "scientific" way of thinking was, therefore, very primitive from our present perspective. So, the question was posed like this:

The proletarian revolution brings the means of production into the ownership of the community, and thus we enter the communist operational life.

Then, however, the laws of motion for individual consumption must absolutely *necessarily* be in accordance with communist operational life, precisely *because* they are inseparably connected with the laws of motion of production. With the transition to communist operational life, this matter, therefore, "regulates itself".

In fact, this is absolutely right!

Only – the transition to "common ownership of the means of production" – does not necessarily lead to the communist operational life!

<u>There is an undeniable urge to state capitalism, and with its implementation, consumption is regulated by the laws of movement of state capitalism!</u>

b. The task of the revolution

This is typically expressed by the representatives of, let's say, state communism. They do not think of establishing a fixed relationship between producer and product. They do not want the worker to determine his relationship to the social product *directly* through his work, even if this would "exclude any exploitation" and prevent any guardianship of a government (see chapter 8a). Rather, they want it to depend on the masters who dispose of the production apparatus **and** the product, how much the worker receives from the social product. **They** will pursue a "pricing policy", i.e., **they** will set the prices for products, and **they** will also conclude collective agreements with the trade unions to fix wages.

How important it is that the workers become aware of the plans that are in the minds of the masters who hope to lead the "communist" economy tomorrow, may become clear from our following considerations. It shows how *absolutely necessary* it is to fight to make the exact relationship between producer and product the *demand of the revolution*.

c. The consumption money

The aim of the revolution is the real abolition of the wage. The social revolution that abolishes wage labor must regulate the relationship of the workers to the social product on new bases. (See chapter 3a)

In other words, *individual consumption must be organized according to new principles.*

The abolition of wage labor has the immediate effect of abolishing the wage. Communism does not know a wage. Here there are only the interconnected producers who struggle **together** against nature to produce consumer goods and then distribute them equally among themselves. Setting working hours as a measure of consumption is nothing more than a technically necessary measure to be able to consume and produce according to plan.

The technical organization of consumption, therefore, requires that workers in the factory receive a "work certificate" (Marx) indicating how many hours they have given to society. These "work certificates" or "labor money" (Owen), or these "consumption certificates" or "consumption money" are, therefore, only an indication of the consumer goods that the workers can freely obtain from the social stocks.

»On this point, I will only say further, that Owen's "labor-money," for instance, is no more "money" than a ticket for the theatre. ... the certificate of labor is merely evidence of the part taken by the individual in the common labor, and of his right to a certain portion of the common produce destined for consumption.«[63]

d. The consumption-money by Leichter

But – if two people say the same thing, it's far from the same. Leichter reaffirms this old wisdom. In his production apparatus with working time calculation, he also introduces the "labor money" for individual consumption, thus creating the impression that work would be the yardstick for this consumption. But this is by no means the case. In his "image of society", as in capitalism, workers are paid according to the value of the labor power. He uses the

---

[63] Karl Marx, Capital Volume 1, p 67, footnote 1

word "labor money" only to disguise capitalist wage relations. He says:

»In truth... the image of society presented here is based on the idea of the allocation of goods "in natura" **in proportion to the work done by each individual***. Labor money is only a form of assignment of the share of the national product chosen for economic-technical reasons.«*[64]

It seems Leichter is saying the same thing as Marx here, but in reality, there is a poisonous snake in the grass. This is reflected in Leichter's peculiar view of *»the work done by each individual«* (see chapter 7e). For him, this means that capitalist wage relations must be maintained, and he uses the term *labor money* only to disguise the perpetuation of wage relations. Producers do *not* get back as many working hours for consumer goods as they have given to society. Still, rather consumption is regulated according to standards that have nothing to do with the calculation of working hours.

But what are these standards?

The "nutritional physiologists" determine how many and which foods *»in a way represent the subsistence minimum«* (Leichter, p. 64), with which then *»the nor-*

---

[64] Otto Leichter, Die Wirtschaftsrechnung in der sozialistischen Gesellschaft, p. 75. Highlighting by GIK

mal, scientifically calculated and balanced life ration« is determined. And that is the basis for the payment. What does this have to do with the calculation of working hours in production?

This minimum is then for the unskilled workers, while the wages of the skilled and semi-skilled workers are set somewhat higher by *"collective agreements"*. Collective agreements determine the basic wage, while *"the socialist factory manager"* sets the wage for individual workers according to their ability.

It is clear that producers can never feel their company as a part of themselves if there are such opposites between them. They can, therefore, never bear the responsibility for the course of production, which is also not what the state communists intend. In Leichter's case, therefore, it is not the producers themselves who are responsible, not the company organization as a whole, but *the director.*

He says that

»any appointed manager of the operational unit bears personal responsibility for him; he can be removed without further ado, just like a capitalist manager who does not meet the demands placed on him. He will then only receive the minimum income guaranteed by society if he is "unemployed", or he will be used in a correspondingly lower and therefore, worse paid position. In this way, the so-called "private initiative" of capitalist managers

and directors and their sense of responsibility, which is also based on their personal interests, can be replaced and preserved for the socialist economy.«[65]

It speaks for Leichter to call it one of the most severe punishments when someone is brought to the subsistence level on a nutritional basis.

e. The wage by Leichter

Although it is clear from the explanations that wage labor is the cornerstone of Leichter's socialism, we will examine wages more closely. To this end, however, it is also necessary to draw attention to "pricing policy". One could believe that at least here, the "socially average production time" should be considered the "price" of products, but this is by no means the case. Leichter is very dark on this point, but it is nevertheless clear that the products enter society in exchange for a higher "price". He speaks, for example, of the "profit", which, however, does not go to the company but to the general treasury (Russia!). These "profits" are then used by the general treasury to provide the funds for the expansion of the operational units.

This "profit fund" is thus shown as an "accumulation fund". We will come back to accumulation

---

[65] Otto Leichter, Die Wirtschaftsrechnung in der sozialistischen Gesellschaft, p. 101. Highlighting by GIK

later, but now we notice that the socially average working time in this production apparatus with working time calculation does *not* find its expression in the "prices" of the products either. The truth is that "production management" determines the prices as it considers it useful and necessary. Thus, it carries out a "price policy".

Thus, capitalist wage relations are irrevocably restored.

As we know, Marx's economy knows three categories of capitalist production in relation to the wage

1. The nominal wage

2. The real or actual wage, and

3. The relative wages.

The nominal wage is the *money price* of labor power. In nutritional communism, this would be the amount of money a worker receives for a week's work, i.e. for a 40 hour week.

The real wage is the quantity of product that can be realized for the nominal wage. Although the nominal wage can remain the same, the real wage becomes higher when the prices of the products fall. For example, falling prices in an economic crisis act as a wage increase for those with "fixed income". Although their wages remain the same, their real wages increase. With the start of a new production cycle, prices usually rise again, thus reducing the real wages of those with "fixed income".

In Leichter's "vision of society", the central management pursues a "price policy", naturally (!) in the interest of the consumers. But this does not change the fact that in reality, IT determines the real wage, despite all "collective agreements," which can only refer to the nominal wage. Producers and consumers may have a say in this pricing policy through "democracy", but the actual conditions, the real pricing policy, are nevertheless determined by the masters of "statistics".

<u>The relative wage</u> is the ratio of the real wage to the entrepreneurial profit. Thus, for example, the real wage may remain the same, while the relative wage decreases because of the profit increases.

In his "social image," Leichter places the greatest emphasis on the rationalization of the operational units, i.e., on more productivity, i.e., the creation of more products in <u>the same</u> or shorter working hours. The socially average time required to manufacture products is thus constantly decreasing. However: the factual relationship between producer and product is not fixed in things for Leichter. Leichter only knows working machines with intelligence that are nourished on a nutritional-physiological basis, which does not need to be fed extra calories as the product mass they create increases. Perhaps the workers also receive some of the greater wealth, but there is not the slightest security for this.

Thus, it is shown that the introduction of the category of socially average working hours in operational life is pointless if we do not, at the same time, take it as a basis for consumption. If the relationship of producers to the product is directly fixed in the things themselves, then there is no room for "price policy", then the result of every improvement of the production apparatus directly falls **automatically** to all consumers, without anyone **assigning** anything.

f. Communism in Soviet Hungary

Leichter is not the only one who seeks his salvation in pricing policy. On the contrary, it is the central point of *all* considerations of communist economic life. More important than all these considerations, however, is practical experience, and that is why we want to examine more closely how the practice of pricing policy and communist operational life took place in Soviet-Hungary. (We do not take Russia as an example because this is not possible in such limited space. In principle, however, it comes down to the same thing).

In "Economic Problems of the Proletarian Dictatorship", the former Soviet-Hungarian People's Commissar Varga explained his experiences and theoretical considerations regarding the Hungarian soviet republic. For the study of communist economics, the history of Hungary is certainly important, because here the theory of state communism was put into practice and practice into theory. In Hungary, communism was built according to the rules of the state communist art and probably under such favorable conditions that the

»transformation and organizational restructuring in Hungary were faster and more vigorous than in Russia.«[66]

The country is much smaller and more densely populated, which made that

»a lot of things could be organized centrally that have to be decentralized due to the huge expansion of Russia.«[67]

The construction took place according to Hilferding's vision of the "general cartel" (see Varga, p. 122), where the state as the general leader and administrator of production and distribution has the full right of disposal over all products. That which was still produced in the "free" capitalist enterprise was bought

---

[66] Eugen Varga, Die wirtschaftspolitischen Probleme der proletarischen Diktatur (The economic problems of the proletarian dictatorship), p. 78
[67] As above, p. 78

up by the state so that the state actually controlled *the total product*.

g. The distribution of the means of production

If the managers have access to the entire social product, they must distribute it, first by making new means of production and raw materials available to the operational units. For this purpose, the Supreme Economic Council had set up various *raw material centers*, which then "allocated" as many raw materials, etc. to the operational units as they deemed useful and necessary. *But these centers were by no means only distribution organs*; they also functioned as political and economical means of power vis-à-vis the working class. These centers had to bring about the concentration of the factories, which was very simple, by simply cutting off factories which one wanted to bring to a standstill "from above" from the supply of materials, which then caused the workforce of the factory to hit the pavement. It is obvious that the workers resisted such a concentration process, which was just as fatal for them in its economic consequences as it was under capitalism.

They were practically taught that the producers did not have the right of disposal over the production apparatus. This right rested with the state officials of the Supreme

Economic Council, which came in irreconcilable opposition to the producers. (See Varga p. 71.)

We want to note that concentration "from above" is probably faster than "from below", but the price that this acceleration cost is the right of the producers to dispose of the production apparatus ..., i.e., communism itself!

h. The pricing policy in Hungary

Turning now to the area of consumption, it should be noted that Varga is basically in favor of an even distribution of the product. This distribution would then take place "in-kind" without a unit of account (see chapter 2d). However, Varga points out that the workers themselves initially rejected an even distribution of the social product and that we must consider a *»generation of workers corrupted by capitalism and educated in a greedy egoistic ideology.«*[68]

We are familiar with this ideology, which makes the skilled look contemptuously at the unskilled, while at the same time, it runs counter to their legal sense that the holders of the intellectual professions, such as doctors and engineers, should not receive a larger share of the social product. There is a certain conviction that the difference is too great today, but ...

---

[68] Eugen Varga, Die wirtschaftspolitischen Probleme der proletarischen Diktatur, p. 42

a doctor is not a garbage collector. The extent to which the workers change this ideology in the course of the revolution remains to be seen. So much is certain that this change must take place quickly after the revolution because an unequal distribution of the product always leads to disputes within the working class itself.

For the distribution of the products the rations for each product were now fixed, which could then be purchased in the cooperatives. »*But since for the time being there are still wages and prices of money*«, we must now turn to the problem of »*the state fixing of prices*« (Varga, p. 147). Varga first states the "solution in principle", which, however, could not be applied. This is then formulated as follows:

»*How high should the price of state products be set? If the state-produced goods were sold at cost price, there would be no income left to maintain the above-mentioned unproductive strata of the population. (This refers to soldiers, civil servants, teachers, unemployed, sick, invalids - GIC). There would also be no possibility of a real accumulation of means of production, which is even more urgently needed in the proletarian state for the purpose of raising the standard of living of the inhabitants than in the capitalist state. In principle, therefore, all state goods must be sold at "social cost price". By this, we mean the cost price plus a supplement sufficient to cover the maintenance costs of the non-working people, plus a supplement to enable real accumulation.* (Highlighting by Varga) *In other words, the selling prices must be determined in such a way that not only does the state not have a deficit, but also a surplus to build new productive operations. This is the principal solution.«*[69]

We will look at this "principle solution" later. We will only point out now that it was not possible to determine the "social production costs" so that a normal pricing policy was applied. In other words, an indirect tax was imposed on various products.

No doubt, Varga wants this pricing policy to be **class politics**, privileging the working class, why he wants to tax the products that are of primary importance to the workers, such as bread and sugar, little, but the "luxury" products highly. However, he attaches more propagandistic than economic importance to this difference in taxation, because he knows very well that the enormous sums which the state devours must ultimately come from the masses, i.e., from the proletariat.

This class politics, however well-intentioned it may be, **reveals the whole rottenness of the state-communist distribution**. *It demonstrates very clearly* that *the producer*, <u>with his work</u>, has **not** at the same

---

[69] Eugen Varga, Die wirtschaftspolitischen Probleme der proletarischen Diktatur, p. 147

time determined his share of the social product, but that this share is determined in the "higher regions" by personal decision.

Thus, the old political struggle for government posts is continued in a new form.

It is clearly shown that whoever has political power in the state also controls the entire social product and, through "price policy", controls the distribution of national income. It is the old struggle for positions of power that is being fought on the backs of the consumers. If we add to this the fact that *wages* are also determined by the Supreme Economic Council (Varga, p. 75), then the picture of state-communist mass slavery is complete.

The central management of production has it entirely in its hands to immediately nullify a forced wage increase through its pricing policy. It is thus evident that in the construction of state communism, the working class creates a production apparatus that rises above the producers, and thus grows into an apparatus of subjugation that is even more difficult to fight than capitalism.

This relationship between the rulers and the ruled finds its concealment in the democratic forms of the distribution organizations. In Russia, a decree was issued on 20 March 1919, which obliged the entire Russian population to form consumer cooperatives.

All these cooperatives, which have their own mobility within their spheres of activity, were then forged into an organic whole. At the same time, the consumers determined the course of distribution by holding meetings and congresses: they were "masters of their own house". Although the state was the stimulating force behind the formation of cooperatives and mergers, once the organization was established, the distribution of the product was left to the people themselves.[70]

According to the "Russian Correspondence", this organizational work of the state should have brought about the enormous distribution apparatus within five months.

This much is certain that the Communist Party dictatorship in Russia has done a tremendous job in this respect, and has set a shining example of how consumers can set up their distribution apparatus in a short time. But if consumers are already "masters of their own house", the question of what communism is all about, namely determining the relationship between producers and the product, is *not decided there*. This decision is made in the central gov-

---

[70] 'Russische Korrespondenz', 20. Jan. 1920. See: Varga, Die wirtschaftspolitischen Probleme der proletarischen Diktatur (The economic problems of the proletarian dictatorship), p. 126

ernment offices. Consumers are then allowed to distribute the product independently, but according to the standards set by the pricing policy.

i. "Fair" distribution?

In communist production, on the other hand, we demand that working time be the measure of consumption. Every worker determines through his work at the same time his share in the social stock of consumer goods. Or as Marx says:

»He receives a certificate from society that he has furnished such-and-such an amount of labor (after deducting his labor for the common funds); and with this certificate, he draws from the social stock of means of consumption as much as the same amount of labor cost. The same amount of labor which he has given to society in one form, he receives back in another.«[71]

This is misinterpreted as a "just" distribution of the social product. And no one can indeed eat with idleness, just as shareholders collect dividends. But that's the end of justice.

At first glance, it seems very fair that all wage differences should be eliminated and that all functions in social life, whether mental or manual, should be given equal rights to the wealth of society. On closer

---

[71] Karl Marx, Critique of the Gotha Programme, part 1

inspection, however, this equal right functions very unfairly.

Take two workers, both of whom give their best to society. But one is unmarried, while the other has a family with five children. Another is married, while husband and wife both work so that they have 'double' income. In other words, the equal right to social wealth becomes a great injustice in practical consumption.

The distribution of goods according to the measure of working time can, therefore, never be derived from equity. The same imperfections stick to the measure of working time as to any other measure. That is to say: there is no fair standard, and it can never exist. Whatever measure is chosen, it must always be unjust. Because using a measure means ignoring the individual differences in needs. One has a few needs, and the other has many. So, one can cover his needs with his assignments to the supplies, while the other has to deny himself all sorts of things. They give all their potential to society, and yet one can satisfy his needs, and the other cannot.

This is the imperfection that is inherent in every measure. The application of a measure of consumption thus becomes an expression of the inequality of consumption.

The demand for equal rights to social wealth, therefore, has nothing to do with justice. Rather, it is a *political demand* par excellence that we as *wage earners* make. For us, the abolition of *wage labor* is the central point of the proletarian revolution. As long as labor is not the measure of consumption, as long as there is a "wage", it may be high or low.

In any case, there is no direct link between the wealth of the goods produced and this wage. Therefore, the management of production, the distribution of goods, and thus the surplus value created, must be transferred to the "higher instances". If working time is the measure of individual consumption, this means nothing other than that wage labor has been abolished, that there is no surplus value creation, and that therefore no "higher instances" are needed to distribute the "national income".

The claim to equal rights to social wealth is, therefore, in no way based on "justice" or any kind of moral evaluation. It is based on the conviction that this is the only way for workers to *maintain* control over operational life. It is on the "injustice" of equal rights that communist society begins to develop.

10.
The general social work

a. Two forms of distribution

In the previous chapters, we have already dealt with the general basis of distribution. As long as goods are still in the production cycle, they are therefore *transferred*, "distributed" based on the socially average production time. When they leave this cycle to move on to individual consumption, distribution takes place on the same basis, with working time being the measure of individual consumption. A single economic law, therefore, regulates the entire operational life, both production and consumption. The same economic law regulates each part of the operational life as well as the whole. Or, as we can also say:

The one general law which governs the whole of operational life – is expressed in every single manifestation of the social metabolic process.

Now, however, we must draw attention to a group of operations which seem to be violating this general law. First and foremost, we are talking about those operations which do not fall within the scope of production but which are nevertheless indispensable to social life. These include, for example, all types of economic and political councils, the economic organizations for general social accounting, health care, education, the creation and maintenance of parks, all types of cultural and social institutions, and so on. The special feature of these operational units is that they do not produce a product, but provide a "service" to society. All these economic organizations consume means of production, raw materials, and food for the workers concerned. Still, for some, it is impossible and for others undesirable to pass on this "service" to the consumer in exchange for work certificates. The nature of these operational units means that they put their "product", their "service", into consumption *without* economic measure. In this way, they work "free of charge" for the consumers, **while at the same time the product is taken according to the needs**. So, we have a group of operational units whose "product" does *not* consider working time as a measure of consumption.

Concerning the distribution of "consumer goods" we, therefore, distinguish between two types of operational units. The first type, which puts its product into consumption in exchange for work certificates, we call **productive operational units**. The others, which work "free of charge", which work according to the principle of "taking as needed", are called

public operational units or **general social work units** (abbreviated as GSW units).

b. The GSW budget

It goes without saying that this difference in distribution brings with it complications in social operational life. "Services" such as health care, education, etc. consume all kinds of social goods, but they do not add a new product to the social stocks. The consequence is that the workers in the productive operational units cannot consume "the proceeds of their labor" on their own. They must also support the workers of the public enterprises, yes, they must also produce the means of production and raw materials for these "services". This is the particular challenge.

For example, if the workers have worked 40 hours a week in their operational unit, they could not get 40 hours of pay, because then nothing would be available for the public service! So, they have to give a part of the proceeds of their work to these services. The question is, however, which part? How much work must they give to public services?

Fortunately, this last question can now be answered very quickly. Public services are invoiced in the same way as productive operational units. They also calculate their consumption of means of production, raw materials, and living labor so that society knows exactly how much labor is consumed by education, health care, and so on. So basically, the same thing happens as under capitalism: the different branches of GSW operations each draw up a budget of how much work they want to spend on the different forms of f, c, and l in the current year. It is the amount of work that the society wants to make available to the public operational units for the current year.

To give this budget a clear representation, we use the same production formula as for the producing operations. However, we put the index p at the foot of the letters to indicate that these are public operational units.

The production formula for each operational unit is thus:

$(f_p + c_p) + l_p$

If we add up the "expenditure" of all public operational units, we have an overview of the total consumption of all public operational units, which we can then simply express with the following formula:

$(F_p + C_p) + L_p$

If we replace the letters with fictitious numbers, the general budget for public services could look like this:

$F_p + C_p + L_p$ = GSW budget

8 million + 50 million + 50 million = 108 million working hours

The question now is how these "social costs" will be borne.

c. The usual solution

The usual solution under capitalism is that the state provides itself with the necessary resources by levying all kinds of direct and indirect taxes, i.e., deprives the consumer of the right to a part of his consumer goods. Russia solves the problem by allowing most of the profits of state enterprises to flow into the state treasury and by levying indirect taxes. For example, by reintroducing vodka (liquor), Russia has acquired the necessary resources, as this has brought several million into the coffers. Soviet-Hungary used the same methods: it obtained the necessary resources through its "price policy", i.e., from the monopoly profits of the operational units and the surplus-value of the labor power.

This is the practical solution.

However, the theory knows two more solutions. First, the solution for the "General Cartel" of Hilferding. In this fantastic fantasy, the subject poses no problem at all. The central control of production determines where the means of production and raw materials should go and, at the same time, allocates to the consumers how much is available for individual consumption. It is true: this theory is rather poor, but we cannot change that.

The second solution is that of calculating the "social cost of production", the so-called "principle solution" of Varga ". He wants to include the "social costs" in the price of the products. But this cannot be called "price policy", because he wants *every* social product to be increased by a fixed percentage. Therefore no "policy" regarding prices can be possible. Unfortunately, Varga does not elaborate on his "principle solution", so we must be satisfied with this feeble reference. However, this theory can easily be followed up with Leichter. We immediately have the advantage that this leads us to an author who knows exactly how to grasp the problem. Later, however, we will see that Leichter gives up his exact solution and again takes pleasure in the "price policy". Finally, we should mention Marx's solution (in the Critique of the Gotha Programme), which does not deal with "pricing policy", which does not include social costs in product prices but gives workers fewer assignments on the social product.

If we summarize both the theoretical and practical solutions, there is a general consensus that costs should be added to the price of the products (except for Marx).

In theory, however, this method is very questionable, as it never gives us a good overview of *»how much work each product requires to make it.«* (see chapter 7b) It, therefore, hinders a proper insight into the rationality of the different operating procedures. Besides, the percentage of prices has to be fixed every year, which leads to "problematic price fluctuations". Moreover, the theorists who want to increase the price of <u>all</u> products will <u>not</u> do so, but will resort to the usual "price policy". Therefore, according to the current state of research on the communist economy, there can be no exact relationship from producer to product. What consumers get out of it always remains an uncertainty. We have to wait and see what is "allocated" to us.

However, we cannot pay enough attention to the fact that this problem is one of the most important issues of communism. That is why, in the face of all the fantasies about the future that are presented to them from different sides, workers must always ask themselves the question: How is the problem of social costs to be solved?

Because this is one of the most important roots of state communism. This is one of the most important roots of the domination of the working class.

The privileged classes will retreat to the fortress of price policy as the last position to maintain their privileges.

d. Leichter' solution

The first one to bring forward the solution to this problem is Otto Leichter because he was the first to put the communist economy on the exact ground of "working time calculation".

The first "source of income" for the social costs lies in the "profits" of companies. This is actually a strange thing with Leichter. Although it is "most obvious" for him to lead the product flow along the path of the "social working time spent on it" (Leichter, p. 38), he does <u>not</u> implement this. Although he groups similar companies to form a "guild", he does not use this to resolve the contradiction between the different operational averages and the social average. (See chapter 8a. Kautskyan Problems.) The production time of the worst, i.e., the "most expensive" enterprise is considered to be the "price" of the product, so that the better-equipped operational units can make an "additional profit", as under capitalism. Of these "profitable" operational units, he says:

»*They will then make a differential rent - or, capitalistically speaking, a surplus profit, which of course cannot be given to this factory alone, but - again, capitalistically speaking - must be taxed away.*«[72]

Of course, these "revenues" are not sufficient, and for Leichter are also not decisive. When he continues to study the subject, he will try to grasp it more precisely, - which is a significant advance over everything we have in this field. Firstly, he wants to add up all general expenses, as we did in our fictitious GSW budget, and then he also wants to determine how many working hours per year are worked together by *all* the workers. (It goes without saying that general social accounting is necessary for this). By comparing these two figures, Leichter believes he has found a figure that indicates how much working time each worker must give to society per hour to cover all social costs. He then creates this "deduction" by increasing the production time of the products according to the number of hours spent on them. Before we explain this in more detail, we will first explain literally what he said about this:

---

[72] Otto Leichter, Die Wirtschaftsrechnung in der sozialistischen Gesellschaft, S. 31

»Each production plant will, therefore, have to reckon with a rate for general administrative costs of the entire factory, to be determined annually when the overall balance sheet, or - in socialist terms - the business plan, is drawn up. ... The total sum of the administrative costs which thus weigh on the entire production will be related to some variable, probably best of all to the total number of hours worked in production and distribution, and the resulting ratio will be added to the wage totals spent when calculating the production costs **so that the cost price of the commodity also includes the costs of society.**«[73]

Because numbers always speak better than words, we want to express Leichter's intention in fictitious numbers.

Leichter asks the question like this:

The GSW budget is 108 million working hours. The total number of hours worked by all workers should be 650 million. Per hour and capita, this results in a social expenditure of $108/650 = 0.166$ hours.

Now the social expenditure must be included in the price of goods. For this purpose, we take our example again from the shoe factory (see chapter 7d). The price by Leichter now looks as follows:

---

[73] Otto Leichter, Die Wirtschaftsrechnung in der sozialistischen Gesellschaft (The economic account in the socialist community), S. 65f. Highlighting by GIK

f + c + l + GSW = price

1,250 + 61,250 + (62,500 × 1.166) = 135,375

This is an average of 3.384 hours per pair.

The "production costs" are now higher than in our calculation, which goes without saying. The "additional income" must now be paid by all operational units to the general treasury, which means that all costs are actually covered.

We have not made this further explanation of Leichter's principle because we agree with it. On the contrary. The wording is wrong. This is shown by the fact that this method of calculation would generate even more than the social costs. However, we do not want to eliminate this "uncleanliness" because we reject the whole principle. The error is because Leichter has no clear idea of what is actually happening. This is evident from the fact that he says that social costs are *probably* best put in relation to work. The reality, however, is that there is no other way!

e. The practical solution by Leichter

However, Leichter's considerations, as mentioned above, are nothing more than a theoretical gimmick for him. He does not take it so seriously. And for those who don't understand it, it's no problem at all, because Leichter doesn't apply it in practice anyway. In practice, he doesn't mind his ratio at all. Yes, he doesn't even look at them! It is even a mystery why he wants it to be calculated. This ratio only makes sense if <u>all</u> products are priced according to <u>this measure</u>. And how does Leichter apply it? Well, as follows:

»*It would, of course, be an injustice and would have almost the effect of an indirect tax if one wanted to add the same general expense rate to all goods, the most primitive as well as the most luxurious, the simplest as well as the most complicated, the most absolutely necessary as well as the most superfluous. It will be one of the* **most important tasks of the economic parliament or the supreme economic management** *to set the general rate of expenses for each industry or product, but always in such a way that the entire expenses of society are brought in. In this way, it will also be possible to influence the pricing policy from central points of view ...*«[74]

To our regret, we have to note here that in Leichter's case, the speech obviously serves to hide the thought. To avoid the accusation of "indirect taxation", he does not want all members of society to bear the costs of education, health, etc. equally,

---

[74] Otto Leichter, Die Wirtschaftsrechnung in der sozialistischen Gesellschaft (The economic account in the socialist community), p. 66. Highlighting by GIC

but apparently wants to draw on those with a "higher income" than those who have been made happy by nutritional physiologists. However, we have to say that, for us, this **indeed** has the character of indirect taxation. We are talking here about the expenses of the **general social institutions**. Why should the rich contribute more here than the physiologically and scientifically nourished?

Is this perhaps Leichter's bad conscience for its antagonistic distribution of the social product?

By the way, we believe with Leichter that it will indeed be one of the most important tasks of the "economic parliament" to determine which products and how much indirect taxes will be levied. Of course! This is a struggle about the distribution of the "national income" and how this distribution will finally come about will be decided by **the balance of power in Leichter's class society!**

It will depend on how much power the working class can develop against the "supreme leadership".

f. The Marxist Solution

When we speak of the "Marxist solution" to the problem, we do not at all mean that Marx gave it to us. Whether or not he has spoken on this subject has nothing to do with it. To make this clear, it should be pointed out at this point that we did not know Marx's most important document on this subject, the »Critique of the Gotha Programme« when we were researching the problems of the communist economy. To solve the problem of "social costs", we had to be guided by the Marxist way of thinking, which confronted us directly with all communist economists. It was only later, after our research was completed, that we got our hands on the »Critique of the Gotha Programme«, and it turned out that our views were completely in line with those of Marx.

In studying the movement of communist economic life, we must be aware that each form of society has its own economic "laws of movement". We found the socially average production time to be the central category that regulates and orders both the economy as a whole and each part separately.

This law of movement also contains a solution to the problem of "social costs". It is certainly "conceivable" that the costs can be found *by the detour of "price increases"*. But then the law of average production time is broken, which leads to all kinds of entanglements in the "international" movement of goods and also (as we will see later) <u>hinders</u> *the growth of communism*. The regulating function of the average production time must be maintained **completely** so that the "social costs" <u>can only</u> be achieved by a *direct deduction* of consumer money. **This is the basic**

solution. Whether this deduction is made directly in the operational unit or is accounted for in some other way is irrelevant.

g. The payout factor

After this principal solution, we can move on to a more concrete consideration. To do this, we must closely follow what actually happens in the distribution of the social product. This is then the following:

Let us imagine, for example, that all goods produced in one year are brought together in one large warehouse. From this social stock, the so-called "productive" companies first take their used means of production and raw materials to be able to start a new production period. Then the "public" companies take as many means of production and raw materials as their budget allows. *The rest is consumed by all workers together.*

This is the essence of *what* actually happens. But of course, *the way* the distribution takes place is not like that. In reality, it does not take place after a year, but at every minute of the day. Nor should it be forgotten that the main characteristic of "productive" operational units is that they do not work "for free" and therefore reproduce themselves. However, they do not have to supply an actual "product" at all. For example, transport companies as long as they are not "public" operational units. All these side effects *obscure* the essential flow of things.

For the time being, we will leave these veils as they are, and we will use figures to illustrate once again the essential process as formulated above. To this end, we assume that the budget for the "productive" operational units is as follows:

$(F + P) + L$ = product mass

100 million + 600 million + 600 million = 1,300 million working hours

From this product mass of 1,300 million working hours, these operational units first renew their means of production and raw materials, *leaving behind a product mass which embodies 600 million working hours*.

The requirements of the public operational units must be covered **from this remainder**. This makes it clear that the "social costs" *can be borne solely by living labor power.*

If we continue with the distribution of the entire social product, we must set up the budget for the social operational units, as already mentioned.

That was:

$(F_p + C_p) + L_p$ = "services"

8 million + 50 million + 50 million = 108 million working hours

According to this budget, public operational units need 58 million working hours to renew their means of production and raw materials. These are therefore deducted from the remaining 600 million, leaving 542 million working hours on products. These 542 million correspond to the individual consumption of *all workers*.

The question now is: How much is that for each worker? To answer this question, we have to determine *what part* of the product each worker receives. This will solve the problem.

All workers together work 650 million hours. (600 million in "productive" operational units) and 50 million in "public" ones. But there are only 542 million working hours left for consumption. So, everyone gets only the 542 / 650 = 0.83 part.

The figure obtained in this way, which indicates what part of their work the workers receive as labor money, we call, in short, the *payout factor*, although it would be better to speak of the *"factor of individual consumption"*. In our example, it is 0.83, which means that a worker who has worked 40 hours receives only 0.83 x 40 = 33.2 working hours of compensation for consumption.

This is the third time we will be dealing with the same subject. First, we gave the "principle solution", then this solution in numbers, and now we will put it into a <u>general form</u>. So, it is always exactly the same but expressed differently. What is the general form of the payout factor?

The problem is the distribution of L. We subtract from it ($F_p + C_p$) so that L - ($F_p + C_p$) remains.

The remainder is distributed over $L + L_p$ working hours, indicating that there are hours available for everyone:

$$\frac{L - (Fp + Cp)}{L + Lp}$$

If we now replace the letters of the formula for the sake of clarity with the concrete numbers of our example and call the payout factor the *Factor of Individual Consumption* (FIC), then it is:

$$\text{FIC} = \frac{600 - 58}{600 + 50} = \frac{542}{650} = 0.83$$

This very simple calculation is possible because all operational units keep accurate accounts of their consumption of means of production, raw materials, and living labor. The general social accounting, which registers the flow of products by simple "transfer", has in a simple way all the data necessary to determine the payout factor. They result from a simple summation in the Giro Office.

In this process of production and distribution, nobody "assigns" anything to anyone. It is not a distribution by persons, but the factual production itself does it. The relationship of the producers to the social product lies in the things themselves. This is then also the explanation of the secret that a state apparatus has no place in production. The whole business life stands on the very real ground because the producers and consumers can manage and administer the whole process themselves, and at the same time, there is no breeding ground for exploitation and oppression. It is only on this basis that the conditions are created for the state to "die off" and take its place in the museum of antiquities, next to the spinning wheel and the bronze ax.[75]

h. The growth process of communism

In our considerations of the payout factor, it is important to keep an eye on the growth process here as well, as it is closely linked to it.

---

[75] Friedrich Engels, Origin of the Family, Private Property, and the State, p. 94
www.marxists.org/archive/marx/works/download/pdf/origin_family.pdf

As a characteristic feature of public operational units, we have mentioned that "taking according to needs" has been achieved here, so that the measure of working time for individual consumption no longer plays a role here. With the growth of communism, this type of operation will probably be expanded more and more, so that also food supply, personal transport (this is also individual consumption!), housing service, etc., in short: the satisfaction of *general needs*, will come to stand on this ground. Of course, it must always be considered in advance whether such a distribution for a particular sector does not involve too great a sacrifice for society. In any case, this is a *process* which, as far as the technical side of the task is concerned, can be carried out quickly. The more society grows in this direction, the more consumer goods are distributed according to this principle, and the less individual work will be the measure of individual consumption. Although working time plays the role of being the measure for individual distribution, *this measure will be destroyed in the course of development!*

In this context, we recall what Marx said about distribution (see chapter 3b):

»The mode of this distribution will vary with the productive organization of the community, and the degree of historical development attained by the producers. We will assume, but

merely for the sake of a parallel with the production of commodities, that the share of each individual producer in the means of subsistence is determined by his labor time.«[76]

What we show in our considerations is that the path of socialization of the distribution of consumer goods is clearly determined. The working time is always only the measure for the part of the social product still to be individually distributed.

This process of socialization of distribution does not take place automatically but is linked to the initiative of the workers. But there is then also room for this initiative. If production is organized to such an extent that a certain branch of industry, which creates a final product for individual needs, runs "smoothly", then nothing stands in the way of integrating this branch of the industry into the public operational units. *All calculations in these companies remain the same.*

Here the workers do not have to wait until it suits the public servants until these gentlemen have sufficient control over the industry. Because each operational unit or complex of operations is a closed unit in the calculation, the producers themselves can carry out the socialization. The production is very flexible due to its own administration.

---

[76] Karl Marx, Capital Volume 1, p 51

In this connection, it should be pointed out that the growth of communism will proceed at different speeds in different places. In one place, the need for "cultural" facilities will be more pronounced than in the other. Through the mobility of production, this difference in growth is also possible. For example, if the workers in one district want to set up several public reading rooms, they can do so without further ado. New institutions are then added, which have a more local significance so that the necessary costs must also be borne by the district concerned. For this district, the payout factor will be changed, which has the effect of a "local tax". In this way, the workers can shape life in its thousand-fold shades themselves.

It is precisely this growth process of communism that makes it necessary for the "social costs" to be determined by a payout factor and not by the detour of "price increases" since this would directly limit self-activity and the shaping of one's own life.

The process of growth from "taking according to needs", moves within fixed limits and is a conscious action of society. In contrast, the speed of growth is mainly determined by the "level of development" of consumers. The faster they learn to economize with the social product, i.e., not to consume it unnecessarily, the faster the distribution will be socialized.

For the calculations of total production, it makes little difference whether there are many or few public operational units. As soon as an operational unit, which used to give its product to individual consumption in return for labor money, changes to the public type, the total budget for public operational units becomes larger and that of "productive" operational units smaller. The payout factor thus becomes <u>smaller and smaller</u> as communism grows. It can probably never disappear completely because it is in the nature of things that only those enterprises that supply *general needs* can change over to the public type. The manifold needs, which arise from the special nature of the different people, will hardly be able to be included in the social distribution. Be that as it may, it is not a matter of principle. The main thing is that the general growth process of communism is firmly established, while the practice of life forms the special shades.

i. Mixed operational units

However, to avoid misunderstandings, it is necessary to point out a complication that the socialization of the distribution for the determination of the payout factor entails. The point is that this socialization also brings into the public domain operational units that do not work exclusively for individual consumption. For example, a power station. As far as it supplies light and electricity to households, it works for individual consumption. However, to the extent that the electricity is transmitted to the various operational units, it functions as a *raw material*. Accordingly, this should be considered when calculating the production time of the products. In other words, the electricity plants **must not** supply "free of charge" here. For this reason, the transport of goods should never be included in the "take as needed" category, as a final product is a consumable only at its destination.

These operational units, which realize "take as needed" for individual consumption and on the other hand, consume their product as a means of production or as a raw material in the production process, are called *mixed operations*. It goes without saying that their number will increase with the increasing socialization of individual distribution.

However, the question now is what complications this will entail for the payout factor since the "social costs do not fully cover consumption by mixed operational units", but only for the part that works "for free".

As soon as the GSW budget also includes mixed companies, it contains, on the one hand, a statement on how many means of production and raw materials are withdrawn from the society and, on the other hand, how many means of production and raw materials are transferred by them in the production process. Through a simple deduction, we then determine how many means of production and raw materials are still covered by the "social costs".

For those who love formulas, we would like to express those mentioned above in the payout factor. And those who don't like it can skip it, because it says exactly the same thing, but only in a different "language".

If we look at the consumption of production resources and raw materials in the GSW budget ($F_p + C_p$) and the amount transferred in production ($F'_p + C'_p$), the GSW budget is only debited with the following amounts

$(F_p + C_p) - (F'_p + C'_p)$

Accordingly, the payout factor:

$$FIC = \frac{L - \{(Fp + Cp) - (F'p + C'p)\}}{L + Lp}$$

11.
The accounting as an ideational summary of the production and distribution process

a. The importance of bookkeeping in general

The accounting of a capitalist enterprise generally has the sense that it must give the entrepreneur an insight into whether he has worked *profitably* or *at a loss*, recording all his income and expenditure or his assets and debts. In addition to this general <u>overview</u>, the individual sections of the accounts give him an <u>insight</u> into all the movements of his assets. When the capitalist checks his company books in his office, he will find there a summary of the production and distribution process of his business. He can see what and how much has been put into the business and what and how much has been taken out. It is important to note that bookkeeping is a completely *passive* function: bookkeeping is nothing more than a kind of photograph of what has happened in the business. It is a kind of miniature mirror that truthfully reflects the events of the huge factories in a concise form. *The bookkeeping is the ideational summary of the company.*

The communist society also has its ideational summary in its books. Here, too, we find an *accurate record of the goods traffic* that flows through the operational unit. On the one hand, we get an overview of the amount of social work that flows *into* the operational unit in the form of raw materials and means of production. On the other hand, we see the quantities of products delivered that *flow out* again.

Besides, we can see how many working hours were required for the transformation process from raw material to product. Or, to illustrate it with the concrete example mentioned above:

$(f + c) + l$

Machines + raw materials + labor = 40,000 pairs of shoes

1,250 working hours + 61,250 working hours + 62,500 working hours = 125,000 working hours

b. Giro transactions as "settlement"

However, as soon as goods are brought into or out of the operational unit, it comes into contact with other operations.

And since it is one of the "lay idea" of capitalism as well as of communism, when one believes that goods can be transferred without charging, the receiving operational unit must "charge" the incoming goods against the supplying operational unit. The question is, *how this is done*. In capitalism, this is done either by direct payment in cash or (and this is the usual way of "settling") by paying the amount through a bank or a giro office. In this case, it is merely a transfer or wiring. The payments are made without the money being put into circulation, it is a "cashless" transfer.

Leichter believes that life practice must decide whether these two forms of settlement should be retained under communism. He says to this:

»All material conditions of production, all semi-finished materials, all raw materials, all auxiliary materials supplied by other production plants to the processing plant are charged, invoiced to it. The question of whether this will result in cash payment with working hours or accounting charges, i.e., "cashless" transactions, will be best solved by practice.«[77]

Indeed, practice will have a decisive say. In principle, however, a payment with working hour money bypassing the giro office is fundamentally wrong. That is why we firmly reject this here since it is a theoretical study. In the course of development, all settlements must be carried out by a central giro office. For just as each individual operational unit

---

[77] Otto Leichter, Die Wirtschaftsrechnung in der sozialistischen Gesellschaft (The economic account in the socialist community), p. 68

needs an ideational representation of its production process, so much more is needed for the entire operational life of the society. If *all settlements* are carried out via the giro, then we have here *a complete record of the goods traffic through the entire society*. It is the general social accounting of the production/distribution process. If, however, some of the settlements take place outside these accounts, we do not have this registration, i.e., we cannot speak of a general social accounting system!

This is one of the reasons why communism must reject direct charging in working hour money, and that is why we do not use the term working money but speak of *consumption money*. This is to express that these "instructions on products" can only be used for the purchase of individual consumer goods and *not* for the settlement between operational units.

c. Transformation of terms: No "income" - no "expenditure"

After these preliminary remarks, we can take a closer look at the communist accounting of the individual operational units. Although it may seem like "hair-splitting" to many, we want to do it because it deepens our understanding of *the essence* of communism. We will see that the accounting terms - profit and loss, income and expenditure, assets, and liabilities - lose their validity under communism.

Even though a large part of these terms will continue to live on in the language of communism, it is necessary to understand that they took on *completely different content*.

To recognize the character of the changes in terms, we must start from the new social relations, i.e., the *new legal order*. In other words, neither the operational unit nor the manufactured product is the property of the operational organization: they are <u>common goods</u> which it manages "in the name of the society". Therefore, the activities of the operational unit cannot be considered as a change in the assets and liabilities of the operational unit and are therefore not linked to actual "income" and "expenses". The operational unit can speak of the quantity of goods which it has taken *out* of the company and which it *transferred* to the society.

Once an operational unit has delivered products, this is recorded in the operational accounting and this amount is transferred from the current account of the receiving operational unit to the account of the delivering operational unit. However, this only means that the society has registered this goods traffic. The amount thus appears in the accounts, but does not have the character of "income". It is a simple registration.

The same applies if the operational unit purchases production means or raw materials from another operational unit. In this case, although it is established how many working hours were spent on this product by the society and although the general giro office transfers this amount to another account, it is by no means an "expense", just as it is not an "income" for the other operational unit. Again, this is merely a registration of the transport of goods. Instead of debit/credit in the current accounting system, the terms should, therefore, be used:

Withdrawn from the Community

> What comes into the operational unit as a means of production or as raw material, expressed in working hours. Also the consumption of consumption money

Transferred to the community

> The quantity of the delivered product.

d. Transformation of terms: No "gain" no "loss"[78]

Just as the operational unit does not have "income" or "expenditure", neither does it have "profits" or "losses". The operational organization only records how much social work it has taken from society in the form of f, c, and living labor and returns the *same amount* to society, but in a *different form*, in the form of the product it produces. *It cannot*, therefore, have "surpluses" or "deficits". We can also express the same phenomenon differently: We can also say that *profitability is unknown!*

But even if the profitability is unknown, the rationality of the operational unit is well known. It may well be that society believes that the quantity of products supplied is too small. This would not mean that the operational unit with a "deficit" would work with a "loss", but it would show that in this unit, the production time of the product would be too high above the social average.

The society or, on behalf of the latter, the operational organizations of the whole industrial sector

---

[78] As always, we assume in this analysis that operational life is running "according to plan" and that there are no additional disruptions. This is the only way to understand the essence of the matter and thus arrive at a clear understanding.

could hold this operational unit *accountable* so that it should explain *why* its production time is so much higher than in other similar operations.

e. The importance of communist accounting

And this brings us to the characteristic difference between capitalist and communist accounting. Both give an ideational summary of the operational unit; however, in the case of capitalism, it is important to determine whether profit or loss has been made. Under communism, on the other hand, it is not only about self-control over the production in the operating unit, but also about the *responsible management of the social goods* that are transferred to society.

f. The general social accounting

The ideational summary of operational life in general social accounting is not an "imaginary" or constructed measure, but the "natural" result of the strict introduction of the average working hours in society as the supporting force of production and distribution. Thus, the whole operational life becomes one, while the recording of the transfer of goods "automatically" gives an overall view of all social activity. In this way, therefore, the general accounts of production and consumption of society as a whole are produced. Here we find an overview of the entire social "inventory" (see chapter 3b) and a description of how it is used.

Of course, there is no information in this "inventory" such as so many drills, so many lathes, so many pickaxes, etc. etc. However, it shows how many means of production each industry uses, how much raw materials and living labor it consumes. In other words, it shows how social work is distributed in a fixed form (means of production and raw materials) and in a fluid form (living labor) among the various social activities. This then also means that all the elements for so-called "planned" production can be found here.

This bookkeeping is bookkeeping in the true sense of the word, and it is *nothing more* than bookkeeping. It is, however, the central point where all the rays of operational life flow together. Still, this economic center does <u>not</u> have the leadership, <u>not</u> the administration, <u>not</u> the power of control over production and distribution. The "operational organization of the general social accounting" has something to say only in its own unit. But this does not result from this or that decree of the Council Congress, nor is it dependent on the goodwill of the workers of the clearing office, but is determined by the course of production itself.

12.
The abolition of the market

a. With the Bolsheviks: The Supreme Economic Council distributes the product of society

The Russian Revolution has not only shown us that production without a unit of accounting is a childish fiction of naive fantasists, but has also given us lively enlightenment on the mysterious, much-discussed question of the "abolition of the market". This has always been a very difficult topic. Yes, Marx was an easy talker! He could say that under communism, the market would be abolished, but how would operational units get their means of production and raw materials if they could no longer obtain them on the market? And how would the workers get their food if the market did not act as a mediator between producers and consumers?

The Bolsheviks are trying to solve the problem by implementing the "General Cartel" of Hilferding. The entire production and distribution would function without money, without a market and without product prices as one huge monster enterprise. The development of the dissolution of the market was very fast because the value of the ruble fell so fast that the prices of goods rose by the hour. Soon almost nothing was available for money so that the entire food supply was almost completely in the hands of the state.

Zinoviev writes about this:

»If the value of money is falling in Russia, it is certainly very difficult for us to bear... But we have a way out, a hope. We're heading for the complete abolition of money. We are naturalizing wages, we are introducing free use of trams, we have free schooling, free lunch, even if for the time being poor, free housing, lighting, etc. We are doing this very slowly, in extremely difficult circumstances, we have to fight all the time, but we have a way out, a hope, a plan...«[79]

In fact, all economic life in the cities was regulated in this way (the farmers were excluded), so that the Commissariat of Food Supply (the Narcomprod) served 38 million people. Considering that telephone, water supply, gas, electricity, rent, transport, and fuel were provided free of charge, it is fair to say that the "market" in the cities was abolished.

It would, therefore, appear that we have an excellent basis here for an investigation into the question of the abolition of the market. However, this is only

---

[79] G. Sinowiew, "Zwölf Tage in Deutschland", S. 74. Quoted by: F. Pollock "Planwirtschaftliche Versuche in der Sowjetunion 1917 – 1927 (The Planned Economy Trials in the Soviet Union 1917–1927), p. 73

the case to a very limited extent, as this "socialization of distribution" had to be carried out under very unfavorable conditions. Russia was shaken by civil wars, which meant that the production system had to be largely geared to war production, and a significant proportion of industrial workers were taken out of production. As a result, farmers could not be supplied with industrial products at all, so they had to supply their grain without receiving anything in return. Under these circumstances, it is obvious that the farmers refused to farm their land so that there was less and less to distribute.

We are giving this information to show that the Russian idea of market abolition had very poor chances of being realized. The fiasco which the concept finally suffered could, therefore, be explained by the supporters of this position from the circumstances. An assessment of the possibility of such a system would only be possible where it could be fully implemented. We would, therefore, only be able to examine the problems of abolishing the market in Russia in practice if we were able to supply farmers with all kinds of products *after all*. Unfortunately, this was not the case, and so the only result is that we have a clear idea of what the Russians mean by abolishing the market. This, in itself, is very important.

The Russian view is as follows:

The Bolsheviks wanted to replace the market with production and consumption statistics. The Supreme Economic Council, in conjunction with Narcomprod, would statistically determine the quantities of bread, sugar, meat, textiles, etc. needed to meet the needs of the population. Accordingly, the Supreme Economic Council would then issue production orders to the operational units. The Supreme Economic Council had an overview of the needs, knew the productive forces and would now set up production to meet the needs of the people. The prerequisite for such production control was that the management and direction of the entire operational life were concentrated in the hands of the Supreme Economic Council.

As we have seen so far, the investigation does not give rise to any new assessments. It is the realization of an old theory that we have already encountered in the discussion about Sebastian Faure's "libertarian communism".

However, the practice has already shown that in such a system, there can be no production calculation in reality (see chapter 2d), so that no planned production can take place.

b. The Supreme Economic Council "distributes" the labor power

However, this practical experience may not be of convincing importance for the workers. Therefore, we will now let the practice speak from a completely different perspective! The practice has already shown that the producers in this system are nothing other than the toy of those who dispose of the means of production and the social product. The Supreme Economic Council is responsible for the distribution of the "national income". It decides which part of the product is intended for the consumer, how much is used to expand the production apparatus – and with which part it strengthens its dominant position in the state apparatus.

Therefore, if it may not yet be convincing to the workers that such production is impossible, the political significance is much more important.

In the ever-increasing concentration of the production apparatus in the hands of the state, **we see the forms in which the dictatorship of the proletariat passes into the dictatorship over the proletariat!**

This is the political lesson we must learn from the Russian "abolition of the market". And it is urgently needed! For among the revolutionary workers, we still find the widespread opinion that the first years of the Russian revolution showed a development towards communism, but that with the introduction of the NEP, with the reintroduction of the market, it was diverted into capitalist channels. Our research shows that this view is *wrong*. The development of the first years was a development towards ever-increasing enslavement of the working class, enslavement that kept pace with the concentration of the productive forces, with the growth of "communism". Every further step towards the supply in "natural produce" meant a greater dependence on the central apparatus. In the end, the situation was such that the production managers had a huge army of slaves at their disposal, and *they* determined how much product they would allocate to this army as wages.

Perhaps many readers will find this formulation exaggerated. But this is by no means the case. We will prove it! This enslavement did not come about because Lenin, Trotsky, etc. were so obsessed with power, *but because there was no other way*. If the management and control of the huge production apparatus are in the hands of a Supreme Economic Council, **then they must have access to the human material!**

The practice of the Russian Revolution proved this. We now want to show how, in this system, all *individual* freedom has ceased, and everyone only has to follow the instructions of the production managers.

Trotsky usually does not mince his words, and so he explains:

»*If we are to speak seriously of a planned economy, if labor is to be distributed in accordance with the economic plan at the given stage of development, the working class must not lead a nomadic life. It must be moved, distributed, and detached, just like the soldiers.*«[80]

The Central Committee for the General Labor Duty, therefore, decided in December 1919 under the chairmanship of Trotsky

»*that the skilled worker leaving the army, with the workbook in hand, in the name of the country's production plan, must go where his presence is required.*«[81]

Besides, the Committee on Labor Duty decided that workers could be forced to give up their homework in order to work in state-owned enterprises, while it could likewise command that

---

[80] L. Trotzki, Russische Korrespondenz 1920, No. 10, p. 12

[81] L. Trotzki, Russische Korrespondenz, No. 8/9, p. 39

»the transfer of labor from one operational unit to another can be carried out in accordance with the production plan...« (as above).

For the introduction of the production plan, the workers were therefore simply sent to work, while they were often forced to work without any remuneration. This was particularly true in the case of logging, where farmers, under the threat of bayonets, were forced to cut wood from the forests without payment. Serfdom was reintroduced under "communism"!

No wonder that the workers did not feel too much for this kind of communism. Thus, Trotsky complains that hundreds of thousands of workers "deserted".

He says:

»In the major industries, we have 1,150,000 workers, but in reality, only 850,000 workers... What happened to the 300,000? They have left. Where did they go? In the village, maybe to other industries, maybe they are engaged in speculation.«[82]

---

[82] L. Trotzki, Russische Korrespondenz, 1920, No. 10, p. 12. The data on the militarization of labor comes from Pollock, p. 57 and 58

We conclude that the practice has already decided that the abolition of the market through a centralized order of production and distribution also means a centralized orientation of the "human material" which, like soldiers, "must be transported, distributed and detached". This also raises the question of whether this is really the "abolition of the market" in the communist sense.

Before we take a closer look at this, let us take a closer look at the Bolshevik view, even if it can't be done on the basis of the practice.

c. The consumption statistics

The real intention of the Bolsheviks, as we know, was to produce for the needs of the workers. Now that is easier said than done. For how will the Supreme Economic Council learn about the needs of the workers? What is its *measure* of need? Surely, it can more or less determine how much bread, meat, etc. is needed by all workers together, so it is relatively easy to produce production and consumption statistics for these matters. However, this has its shortcomings, because it is very complicated to consider the shades of needs in statistics. This makes it even more difficult to go beyond the uniform bread, uniform clothes, and the uniform sausage. The objections become even more serious, however, if we look at the products that are not used by everyone, but which are due to the special nature of different people. How great is the demand for these goods? Surely the statistician can try – but that is precisely not to gear production to the needs of people. And last but not least, there is the major objection that if you produce according to statistics, you make economic life freeze. If operational units have produced according to consumption statistics, it is very likely that demand has already changed again, and therefore the apparatus is *not* geared to demand.

The thing is, therefore, that it is not possible to squeeze the flow of life into the formulas of the consumption statistics, and it, therefore, makes no sense to want to determine demand statistically. Statistics do not go beyond the very general: they cannot grasp the particular. We can, therefore, say that production according to consumption statistics is by no means production according to needs, but rather production according to certain standards, which for us are determined by the central management body of operational life.

But as we have already said, this is an academic question. After all, we are not interested in whether production based on statistics is possible or not. In any case, it can only be carried out if there is a central power of disposal over the "human material", and we do not want that.

d. With the bourgeois economists. The market as a measure of needs

For the bourgeois critics of communism, the "abolition of the market" is the central point of their struggle and also their strongest weapon. It is no coincidence that this is their strongest weapon. In the struggle against communism, they can only oppose the hitherto prevailing conception of communism, which is nothing other than the replacement of the market by a statistical apparatus. The critics rightly point out that these are hollow phrases that conceal the lack of clear concepts.

The bourgeois critics all agree that the market, despite all it's negative aspects, is in any case a *measure of needs*. The market "playfully" solves the question of adapting the production apparatus to needs. The "market mechanism" ensures that a change in requirements is immediately transferred to the production system without the use of statistics. When the demand for a certain product increases, the demand on the market increases, prices rise, and the capitalists expand the production for this item. When the demand for a particular product decreases, the market immediately reduces production to match the reduced demand. From their point of view, the "market mechanism" can very well do what the consumption statistics cannot do.

Therefore they declare communism to be impossible as long as it cannot be specified what is to replace this "mechanism".

The economist H. Block formulates this as follows:

»*If the individual exchange is abolished, the production is necessarily social, so the products are necessarily social as well. Marx did not continue to rack his brains over the methods of achieving and determining social necessity. ... As long as it cannot be shown how the market mechanism is to be replaced, an economic calculation in the common economy, i.e., rational socialism, is unthinkable.*«[83]

Before we deal with this topic, we must consider the difference in character between capitalist and communist distribution. It is true that the market is an indicator of needs – but only in the capitalist sense. The thing is that labor power is a "commodity" that can be bought on the market, while the price is about the minimum subsistence level. The national product can grow immensely, but the worker receives no more than the quantity determined by the value of his labor power. Without a doubt, his needs are much greater; they are just awakened by the great mass of product that is unattainable for him.

---

[83] H. Block, Die Marx'sche Geldtheorie (The Marxist Theory of Money), p. 121-122

Let capitalism, with a beautiful gesture, point to its market mechanism, which is supposed to be an indicator of need; *in reality, it does not know needs*, or even less so than those who want to replace the market with a statistical apparatus. It is not even necessary for capitalism to know needs, precisely *because it does not create for needs but profit*. Capitalism works best, and it is "healthiest" when real big profits are made, that is when the workers are given as little as possible. For the proletariat, the whole splendid market mechanism moves only within the narrow limits that capitalist profit production leaves to the "commodity" labor power. At the same time, there is no question of knowing the needs in the communist sense.

e. The abolition of the market in the Marxist sense

So far, we have not made any further progress on the question of market abolition. We will, therefore, examine the Marxist view of the "abolition of the market".

The market is the place where the owners of the products meet to exchange their "commodities". It is thus through the market that the transport of goods between companies is carried out and the distribution of consumer goods is carried out. This movement and distribution of goods must *also* take place under communism so that it is not a specific capitalist phenomenon. This cannot, therefore, be the abolition of the market.

The market, however, does *not only* provide for the distribution of goods but *at the same time,* expresses the social conditions in which we live. It expresses the fact that the *goods* are privately owned. The market is also an expression of ownership. **That** is the essence of the market.

Under communism, the market is simply abolished because –

»under the altered circumstances, no one can give anything except his labor, and because, on the other hand, nothing can pass to the ownership of individuals, except individual means of consumption.«[84]

This is the famous suspension of the market! The abolition of the market is in the Marxist sense nothing more than the result of the *new legal relations*. It says nothing about the organization of production or consumption or how production is linked to needs. Bolshevism regards the abolition of the market as an organizational question: how can all oper-

---

[84] Karl Marx, Critique of the Gotha Programme, part I

ational units be united in one hand? With the abolition of the market, Marxism expresses *only* the change in social relations, the change in ownership.

As already mentioned, the movement of goods naturally remains under communism. However, the price of goods is not determined by supply and demand but moves on the basis of their production time.

In the "Association of Free and Equal Producers", therefore, the various operational organizations must interact with each other if they wish to receive goods. Since there is "settlement" between the operational units, it looks as if it is a matter of buying and selling, and thus the market still *seems* to be present.

The same applies to the distribution of consumer goods. Consumers receive their products in their cooperative for consumption money and have complete freedom in the choice of goods. So here too, it *seems* as if they buy and sell, although it is no different than redeeming consumer vouchers for products. It can also be said that consumers have several vouchers with which they can collect the goods of their choice.

The abolition of the market can, therefore, be understood to mean that it continues to exist under communism, *according to its external appearance*. However, the social **content** of the movement of goods has changed fundamentally: *The transmission* of goods based on production time is an expression of the new social conditions.

In fact, this is a transformation of concepts, as we have seen previously in terms of value, income, and expenditure, etc. And just as language will preserve all these old names for the time being, it will also preserve the name "market", because *»obviously, the same principle prevails as that which regulates the exchange of commodities, as far as this is exchange of equal values,«* but *»content and form are changed ...«*[85]

f. The orientation of production to the needs

However, the economist, Block, is not satisfied with such an explanation of the abolition of the market, because it does not solve the problem he is actually talking about. He wants to know what will replace the "market mechanism," what is the measure of needs under communism, that is, how the production apparatus will be adapted to needs. We answer that capitalism has *no* measure of needs, and therefore we don't have to "replace" anything at all. Com-

---

[85] Karl Marx, Critique of the Gotha Programme, part I

munism can only achieve this by linking the distribution organizations directly to production so that needs become the direct guideline of production.

Thanks to the triple-sanctified market mechanism which supposedly adapted production to needs, the proletariat, when it takes power, is burdened with a production apparatus which unproductively squanders at least half of the labor power. At the same time, it is set up *not* according to the needs of millions but according to purchasing power.

»Of the workers who are involved in the production of consumer goods, a greater part will produce those articles which serve the consumption of the capitalists, landowners and their retinue (state officials, church people, etc.); only a small part will produce those articles which are intended for the consumption of the income of the working class. ... With the change in the social relationship between worker and capitalist, with the revolutionary transformation of the capitalist relations of production, this would change immediately. ... If the working class is at the helm, if it has the power to produce for itself, it will very quickly and without much effort raise capital (to speak with the vulgar economists) to the level of its own needs.«[86]

---

[86] K. Marx, Theories of Surplus Value, Vol. II, p. 376 quoted by: Varga p.49

The adjustment of production to the needs, therefore, involves a complete transformation of the production apparatus. The factories that work exclusively for the luxury needs of the bourgeoisie are coming to a standstill or must be directed to the needs of the workers as quickly as possible. How quickly such a transformation can take place, we have seen during the war and in the following years in all countries. First, the whole production apparatus was adjusted to the production of war material, only to be transformed again after 1918 for the "products of peace". By the way, it should be noted that capitalism itself switched off its famous "market mechanism" when it set up production for **its** needs, the needs of war.

The organizational transformation into a communist economy can be carried out quickly despite the enormous difficulties whereby the needs for clothing, food, and housing are the guiding principles for the transformation. The food and drink industry is being transformed in such a way that the products that were previously produced exclusively for the bourgeoisie are no longer being made because the focus will be the satisfaction of the needs of the proletariat. Housing construction is a burning issue for the working class. A large part of production must, therefore, be directed towards the production of materials for housing construction. In short, the whole production undergoes a thorough transformation to meet the new demands.

The first stage of communist production will, therefore, be characterized by the strong growth of some industries and the shrinking of others. It is a transformation process that will certainly not be without problems and inconveniences. It must therefore also be emphasized that this construction cannot simply take place in an uncontrolled manner, but that it must be carried out "systematically". In this respect, the various efforts that have been and are being made to this end in Russia undoubtedly provide valuable material. While it is true that the Russian economy is based on the profitability of state capital and **not** on the needs of the workers, it is the only practical experience we have in this field, and we must make use of what we have.

g. The cooperatives and the "benchmark" of needs

The needs are, therefore, the driving force and the guideline of communist production. Or, as we can also say, production is geared to "demand". But not the "demand" in the wild, as capitalism knows it. We must not lose sight of the fact that production and distribution are by no means independent of each other, but that they determine each other. That is why the "union of free and equal producers" also requires the "union of free and equal consumers". Just as production is carried out collectively by the operational organizations, distribution is carried out collectively by *all kinds of cooperatives*. In these cooperatives, the individual wishes of the consumers are expressed jointly. And because under communism, the "middlemen" disappear and the cooperatives are directly linked to the operational units, the needs, as they are expressed in the cooperatives, are *directly* transferred to production.

Undoubtedly, since the current production system is so badly adapted to needs, it will certainly not be possible to satisfy needs in the first days of communism. Now the operational units are not supposed to expand production on their own authority in order to be able to react quickly to incoming orders because they cannot go beyond the general framework established in the general production plan. They can move freely but within the plan. Otherwise, other sectors will run into difficulties, so that a targeted conversion is not possible.

This link between the production apparatus and needs is an issue that can only be resolved by the flow of life, with the production plan as the guide for the producers' own initiative and activity.

Just as the liberation of the workers can only be the work of the workers themselves, it is also self-evident that the organizational connection between production and needs can only be the work of the producer-consumer.

13.
The expansion of production

a. The simple reproduction as the starting point

However, the adaptation of production to needs brings a separate issue into focus, which we must consider here. It is a matter of expanding old, existing operational units and creating new ones; in other words, it is a matter of *expanding* the production apparatus, or "accumulation". This expansion raises various problems for the distribution of the social product, which we have not considered so far.

To make it possible to study the laws of movement of communist operational life, we started from a social situation that will never occur in practice. We assumed that all operational units would produce on the same basis every year. In other words, we assumed that the production apparatus would **not** be expanded. As a starting point, we assumed that each year only the wear and tear would be compensated, and the rest of the social product would be used for consumption.

Our example was the following:

The total wear and tear of all means of production are 108 million working hours, the raw materials

650 million working hours, and the work of all workers together also 650 million hours. The total product is then:

$(F_t + C_t) + L_t =$ Total Product or

108 million + 650 million + 650 million = 1,408 million working hours

This product mass is now distributed to operational units and consumers as follows (see chapter 10g)

1. The productive operational units use it for their wear and tear and their new raw materials 700 million.

2. Public operational units take their wear and tear and their new raw materials 58 million.

3. Consumers use as much as their hours worked 650 million.

The total stock of goods 1,408 million.

(NOTE!)

(Concerning this stock of goods we must not only think of "material" things. It also includes "immaterial consumer goods" (theatre performances, exhibitions). This production is also based on the normal calculation of the consumption of working time $(f + c) + l =$ theatre performance. The workers who take part in such a performance can "consume" it by paying with their consumption-money, at least as far as this kind of service is not yet covered by "taking as needed". Our concept of the "stock of goods" therefore includes the result of all social work.)

The distribution of the "national income" to the three groups of consumption we have mentioned (1, 2, 3) is not the result of a central bureaucratic apparatus which manages and controls the production apparatus and the social goods, but this distribution comes "by itself" since the operational organizations replenish their wear and tear and their raw materials. The same applies to consumption. Since working time is the <u>measure</u> for the distribution of social products, the entire distribution falls outside any "politics". As a result, the <u>trade unions</u> have <u>no function</u> under communism: the struggle for the "improvement of working conditions" is over. The *objective course* of operational life decides **itself** how much product is returned to the production system and how much each employee receives for consumption. It is the self-movement of operational life.

After we have become aware of this, of what actually happens through the definition of working time as a measure of consumption, we can move on to the question of the *expansion* of the production apparatus. We must therefore now move away from our provisional assumption that all operational units will continue production on the same basis. An expanding operational unit **not only** needs to replenish its worn parts and raw materials but **in addition,** it needs to absorb <u>more</u> production resources and raw materials.

b. The expansion of production is always at the expense of consumption

However, the above production plan shows that the goods required for the extension of the apparatus are not available!

The entire social product has already been consumed. Therefore, it is necessary to make additional efforts for the expansion. For example, the working time would have to be extended by 5 hours per week, which would then be used exclusively for the expansion of the operational unit. In other words, we cannot exploit the "full yield of our work", but must "save" part of it. The expansion of the operational unit is, therefore, always at the expense of social consumption. The speed of the expansion of operational units will, therefore, be one of the main points of discussion under communism, since this speed determines the length of the working day, or in other words: This speed determines how much product is left for consumption. It now depends on how this reduction in consumption is achieved and how these "costs" for the expansion of the operational units can be determined.

c. The general rule for the expansion of the operational unit

The general rule, which applies in Russia and in Soviet-Hungary, is that the prices of the products are set so high that the operational units make enough profit to be able to carry out the expansions. Direct and indirect taxes also contribute to this. Russia is an excellent example of how operational life is not influenced by the decisions of the workers themselves, but is entirely in the hands of the ruling bureaucratic caste. As far as we have already looked at this method of "price policy" in dealing with general social work, we need not go into it again now.

But how does the "Association of Free and Equal Producers" find a solution to the problem of "accumulation"? This solution is determined by the essential task of the social, proletarian revolution.

According to our (and we say Marxist) conception, the real task of the proletarian revolution is the implementation of **generally valid rules** according to which producers and consumers, organize production and distribution themselves independently. As far as production is concerned, we have established as a general rule that **all** operational organizations should calculate the production time of their product. As far as consumption is concerned, we have established as a general rule that working time will be the measure of consumption. Since the management of the operational unit is a function of the producers themselves, the third general rule to be added is a fixed rule for the extension of the operational unit. With the implementation of these rules, all producers will participate in the production process under the *same economic conditions* and will thus become **equal** producers.

If we now take a closer look at the general rule on the expansion of operational units, it should be noted at the outset that we are not primarily guided by economic but by political considerations when dealing with this issue. The solution to **all** the problems of the communist economy must be dealt with from the point of view that the workers themselves have control over the economy. Certainly, there can often enough be a contradiction between this independent administration and more rational production. In such cases, we work less "rationally" and then accept a slower development of operational life. If we deviate from our demand for independent management, a bureaucratic caste will soon take over the management of the operational units, which will soon move to what they consider to be a more "just" distribution of "national income". This is why the question of the expansion of the operational units must also be dealt with from the point of view of independent management.

To transfer the needs of workers directly to production, it was necessary to link consumer organizations directly to production. This also means, however, that operational organizations must be able to expand their operations if this is necessary to meet needs. They should, therefore, have the **right** to expand their stocks. The transformation of social relations, therefore, leads to new **legal relationships** in this area too.

However, the expansion of the operational unit cannot take place arbitrarily, as in this case there can be no question of a social production system. The general congress of works councils will, therefore, have to set a certain general standard within which the expansion must take place. For example, congress can stipulate that the operational unit may not be expanded by more than 10% of the means of production and raw materials.

This simple decision will then regulate the entire economic life as far as the expansion of the operational units is concerned,

without the producers becoming dependent on a central economic authority. Every operational organization now knows exactly how far it can go without disturbing the social calculation of production. If we look at the example of the shoe factory already used, production is calculated as follows:

$(f + c) + l = 40,000$ pairs of shoes

1,250 working hours + 61,250 working hours + 62,500 working hours = 125,000 working hours.

This is an average of 3.125 hours per pair.

The operational unit now has 10% of the production equipment and raw materials available for the expansion of the plant, i.e., 10% of 62,500 corresponds to 6,250 working hours.

The following year, an amount of 62,500 + 6,250 working hours appears in the accounts of the operational unit and in those of the General Social Accounts under the heading "Taken from society".

If all the operational units now use their rights, they are all increased by 10%, which means that the entire production system has been increased by 10%.

This is the production comparison for the current year:

$(F_t + C_t) + L_t =$ total production,

then it will be for next year:

$1.1 \times (F_t + C_t) + L_t =$ total production.

d. The application of the general rule

Such a decision, for example, to provide for a general extension of a maximum of 10 %, aims only to regulate production and consumption in broad terms in order to determine broadly how much product can be withdrawn from consumption without causing a disturbance. The sole purpose of this is to ensure the mobility of operational units so that producers can actually adapt production to their needs. It is clear, however, that not every operational organization will have to exercise its right to expand its activities, as several sectors will be able to meet all requests. On the other hand, there are other industries (housing, food industry) that are still far from being able to meet their needs for the time being. Such industries require a far greater expansion than 10% of the consumption of production means and raw materials. However, they must not go beyond the general requirements, as this could lead to supply problems. However, it is quite possible that, especially in the initial phase, several operational units will transfer their right of expansion to such "needy" industries, thus providing them with a larger expansion fund.

In any case, it is *essential* that the operational organizations ensure that they have the **right to extend** if this is necessary to meet demand. On this basis, many organizational forms are possible, which ensure a regular production flow. *How* the economic principle is organized can only be solved through practice; it depends on the circumstances in which the working class comes to power *and* on the type of operational units. The organization of the operational life and especially a rationally planned production does not exist at the beginning of the revolution but takes shape in the process of development. The revolution destroys the old social relations and creates new laws of movement for the movement of goods. The organizational *social* control of operational life grows with the new laws of movement. The organizations are constantly changing manifestations in which the general, social basis is reflected again and again.

e. The influence on the payout factor

We have already seen above that, in our opinion, the costs of expanding the operational units cannot be recovered through "profits" of the units, i.e., through any kind of indirect taxation. The basis for the transport of goods is and remains the socially average production time of the products. The reduction of consumption can, therefore, not be found by way of "price policy", but must be achieved by a *direct* reduction in consumption.

How much does each worker have to contribute to this expansion of the operational unit?

For those who have carefully followed our considerations on the payout factor, the solution is very simple.

For the total production, we had assumed

$(F_t + C_t) + L_t$ = Total production

108 million working hours + 650 million working hours + 650 million working hours

The cost of the plant expansion is now 10 % of (F_t and C_t) 10 % of 758 million working hours equal to 75.8 million working hours. This amount must be paid by all employees together so that 75.8 / 650 = 0.12 of their consumption.

According to our calculation, the payout factor *without* operational expansion was 0.83 (see chapter 10g). This is now 0.83 - 0.12 = 0.71 *with* operational expansion. For a working week of 40 hours, everyone receives 0.71 x 40 = 28.4 hours of consumption.

f. Special accumulation

In addition to the usual accumulation, we will also look at the special operational expansion. By this, we mean the realization of larger works that will take several years, such as the construction of bridges and railways, the completion of transport routes, the construction of sea walls, the reclamation of wasteland, etc. These works usually take several years. Such activities also reduce the quantity of the product for individual consumption. As long as, for example, a railway is being built, all kinds of tools and raw materials are used, but for the time being no new product will replace them. Moreover, the workers who work on it are taken out of normal production, so they too consume, but do not return any products during these years. This kind of expansion of production absorbs a significant proportion of the social product, from which it follows that an important part of the discussions at the economic congresses of the worker's counsels must deal with the questions *to what extent* these works should be initiated and which ones are the most urgent. The higher the productivity of the work process, the easier we can satisfy our needs respectively realize the special accumulation on a larger scale.

»If we conceive society as being not capitalistic but communistic, there will be no money-capital at all in the first place, not the disguises cloaking the transactions arising on account of it. The question then comes down to the need of society to calculate beforehand how much labor, means of production, and means of subsistence it can invest, without detriment, in such lines of business as for instance the building of railways,

which do not furnish any means of production or subsistence, nor produce any useful effect for a long time, a year or more, while they extract labor, means of production and means of subsistence from the total annual production. In capitalist society, however ... great disturbances may and must constantly occur. On the one hand pressure is brought to bear on the money-market, while on the other, an easy money-market calls such enterprises into being en masse, thus creating the very circumstances which later give rise to pressure on the money-market. Pressure is brought to bear on the money-market, since large advances of money-capital are constantly needed here for long periods of time. And this regardless of the fact that industrialists and merchants throw the money-capital necessary to carry on their business into speculative railway schemes; etc., and make it good by borrowing in the money-market.«[87]

Therefore, if it seems desirable to build a new railway, a budget must first be drawn up, stating how much social product (i.e., how many working hours) this will take up in total and over how many years it will be distributed. The character of this work is that it belongs to the type "public", i.e., it burdens the budget for general social work (GSW). Although this reduces the payout factor, the costs of such an

---

[87] Karl Marx, Capital Volume 2, Chapter 16 III, https://www.marxists.org/archive/marx/works/1885-c2/ch16.htm#3

expansion of the operational unit are borne by society as a whole, without breaking the link from the producer to the social product. Once the work has been completed, it can be transferred to the administration and management of the operational organization, which will now carry out the normal operational calculation. In this way, it can be transferred to the "productive" type of operation, for example, if required.

g. The general fund

Finally, we would like to point out a circumstance that also influences the payout factor. This is the need for society to stockpile various products in order to be able to provide support in the event of natural or technical disasters. We are thinking here of major floods, hurricanes, peat fires, etc., where the victims are dependent on the help of a "private charity". Under communism, this type of hardship will have to be borne by the whole of society, so it is natural that a "general fund" should be set up with the help of the payout factor. The speed with which this stockpiling is carried out is in the hands of the councils, which must determine the amount of this fund at the congresses.

14.
The control of the operating life

a. The beginnings of workers' control in the Kerensky era

The Russian and Hungarian revolutions have also raised the question of production control in practice. If we now take a look at what was meant by "production control", it immediately becomes clear that very different things were combined, so that we first have to look at what the meanings behind them were.

For the Bolsheviks, apart from the demand for peace, the central point of the program with which they began the revolution was the control of production by the workers. Operational life, which was increasingly disrupted by the war, could not be brought back into normal tracks by Kerensky's Social Democratic government. The inflation of money had a devastating effect on the purchasing power of the masses, there was a lack of raw materials for the various factories, while hoarders and speculators could use the general chaos to make unprecedented profits at the expense of the working people.[88]

Under these circumstances, a movement arose among the workers, especially in Petrograd, who did not want to simply surrender to the decisions of the entrepreneurs. The works councils often fought against the dismissal of workers or the closure of factories. In June 1917, they demanded to be able to inspect the books of a company for the first time to ensure that raw materials were leaving the factory "not without reason". In October, a metal factory wanted to reduce the size of the factory "due to lack of material", at which point the works council took the right to inspect the books, while each order had to be signed by the management and also by the representative of the works council. In general, it can be said that this movement demanded the right to co-determination in the hiring and firing of workers, in the setting of prices and in many cases the involvement of workers in the day-to-day management of the factory. Sometimes they also demanded

---

[88] See here, for example, V. I. Lenin, How the Capitalists Conceal Their Profits. Concerning the issue of control" in Lenin Collected Works, Vol 25, pages 140-141, Marxists.org, https://www.marxists.org/archive/lenin/works/1917/jul/12a.htm

the dismissal of a particularly hated director or certain manager. In short, it can be said that *they demanded worker-participation*. It should be stressed that the trade unions, which were only founded in the course of 1917, did not belong to this movement at all. The demand for worker-participation was the result of the energetic initiative, the self-determination of the workers, and such a movement could obviously not be carried out by trade union officials. On the other hand, however, it should be noted that the struggle was *not* about the expropriation of the owners, i.e., the abolition of capitalism: the control of production meant only *the control of the capitalists.*

To illustrate this, we give below statistics on the number of directors and managers who had to be dismissed in 1917 under the pressure of the workers.[89]

Month	Number
March	59
April	5
May	-
June	4

---

[89] Friedrich Pollock, *Die planwirtschaftlichen Versuche in der Sowjet-Union 1917-1927* (The Planned Economy Trials in the Soviet Union 1917–1927), p. 25, Leipzig, 1929. [This source is not mentioned in the original]

July 5

August 17

September 21

The Menshevik Labor Minister Skobolev, of course, could not allow this movement to continue. So he gave the order that works councils should not interfere in the management of the factory. That was water on the mills for the Bolsheviks. They used the elementary movement for factory control in their propaganda to organize the works councils in a federal context. The fact that when in revolutionary Petrograd power was taken over, only 30% of the works councils were organized in the unions shows how little these works councils coincided with the unions. Later, when the Bolsheviks came to power, the scope of factory control was established by the November 14 decree, which established as *legal rights* the various actions of the workers that were previously considered illegal. (We will come back to this later).

b. The "workers' control" by Marx

It is one of Lenin's great merits that he (before the Bolshevik coup on November 7, 1917) in his pamphlet "State and Revolution" clearly pointed out the changes in the ideas of communism that Marx had undergone over the years. In the Manifesto of the

Communist Party (1847), Marx sees the development of communism in ever more far-reaching state capitalism, as we can see it today in Russia.[90]

The working class takes over the bourgeoisie's governing apparatus, and the new governing party (parties?) will then carry out a radical *reform program* with the help of this old apparatus. In the "Communist Manifesto", the implementation of communism is *not* the task of the revolutionary masses. The expropriation of the owners is brought about by the new government, which "gradually snatches all capital" from the bourgeoisie. Land ownership is abolished, but the peasants must, as in the past, raise the ground rent, which is then due to the state. Private capital is still functioning for the time being, but the owners must pay *"heavy progressive taxes"*. The national credit bank receives a *credit monopoly*, and a state transport monopoly is also introduced. Then the state will begin to expropriate more and more companies in order to put them into state operation, while at the same time there must be a rapid increase in the number of "national factories". (In Russia, the five-year plan.)

---

[90] K. Marx, F. Engels, Manifesto of the Communist Party www.marxists.org/archive/marx/works/download/pdf/Manifesto.pdf, p. 26f

The revolutionary movements of 1848, and in particular the Paris Commune (1871), strongly criticized this radical reform plan. Marx himself, therefore, concluded that the practice of class struggle had shown that these views were wrong for the developed capitalist countries. In 1871, in particular, it became clear that the revolutionary masses not only had to expel the old rulers but also had to destroy the military-bureaucratic state apparatus. Thus, Marx concluded in his Civil War in France that the working class cannot take over the state from the bourgeoisie, but that it must "*destroy*", "*smash*" the state.

What is this "smashing" of the state? The state is not a porcelain vase to be broken. If you want to smash the state, you must neutralize the military-bureaucratic caste that rises above the masses like a thousand-headed monster. The Paris Commune did this by introducing *full self-government*. It did not recognize the civil servants appointed by the central government but reserved the right to appoint and dismiss *all* civil servants itself. As a result, they were no longer accountable to the central state authority, but only to those who had delegated them. The revolutionary masses had taken over the legislative **and** executive power. There was no longer a bureaucratic caste cut off from the masses, but the officials themselves had become a living part of the masses.

The right of appointment and dismissal by the members of the commune itself placed *all* officials *under the control* of the masses: they became the real executive organs of the masses. The Commune

»*in this first place, it filled all posts – administrative, judicial, and educational – by election on the basis of universal suffrage of all concerned, with the right of the same electors to recall their delegate at any time. And in the second place, all officials, high or low, were paid only the wages received by other workers..*«[91]

The general introduction of the principle of "accountability downwards" is, in reality, nothing more than the fact that the *direct* management and direction of all social life has passed into the hands of the workers, without taking the detour via the state. The general implementation of this principle is also in direct contrast to the state-capitalist ideas of "nationalization" of "mature" enterprises. From this conception, it is clear that society *as a whole* is "mature" for communism in the Marxist way of thinking and therefore moves *as a whole* to the new mode of production.

---

[91] Friedrich Engels, Introduction to The Civil War in France,
www.marxists.org/archive/marx/works/1871/civil-war-france/postscript.htm

The propaganda that the communist parties use to present the gradual takeover of enterprises by the state as growth towards communism is extremely destructive for the development of the *communist orientation* of the working class. It does not focus on the awareness that the working class must take direct control of social life but serves only as a tool to help the communist parties gain power in government. Then "communism" is gradually implemented from the governmental authorities under the dictatorship of the Communist Party.

However, in the highly developed capitalist countries, a real proletarian revolution cannot take place along these lines. The implementation of a revolution means that the revolutionary energies of the masses are released. And these masses are so numerous (unlike in Russia) that the destructive and constructive forces cannot be kept within the decrees of the government parties. In a real proletarian revolution, a party dictatorship cannot assert itself. A party dictatorship can only be successful if the revolution *does not* go on if it gets stuck halfway. A party dictatorship only gets a chance as the product of an unfulfilled revolution, to which the bourgeoisie joins as a last resort "to prevent worse", because a party dictatorship can at best achieve state capitalism, i.e., it allows capitalism to continue, albeit in a modified form.

c. Worker Control among the Bolsheviks

The course of the Russian Revolution practically shows the incompatibility between the "Communist Manifesto" and the "Civil War in France". Or, in other words, the *practice* has shown that the principles of the Paris Commune, "responsibility downwards", i.e., the rule of the working class, are incompatible with state capitalism. The Bolsheviks wanted to unite the two, which proved impossible: they increasingly had to take the leadership of social life out of the hands of the workers to transfer it to the old bourgeoisie and the central government agencies.

When the Bolsheviks came to power, they implemented the measures outlined in the Communist Manifesto. Only the banks and the transport sector were to be taken over by the state, while industry was to remain in private hands.

»We see a sample of state capitalism in Germany. ... But if you reflect even slightly on what it would mean if the foundations of such state capitalism were established in Russia, Soviet Russia, everyone who is not out of his senses ... would have to say that state capitalism would be our salvation.«[92]

---

[92] V. I. Lenin, Session of the All-Russia C.E.C, Report On The Immediate Tasks Of The Soviet Government, collected works vol. 27

In the CPR, there is the only disagreement about the pace at which this state capitalism is being implemented. The "Left", led by Radek and Bukharin, is pushing for the immediate transfer of industry to the state, but Lenin can stop this by the end of June.

That it was indeed *not* the intention to expropriate the bourgeoisie is evident from Lenin's pamphlet "The Imminent Catastrophe". This brochure was written a month before the revolution. Here Lenin addresses the issue of *nationalization of banks* and says:

»If nationalization of the banks is so often confused with the confiscation of private property, it is the bourgeois press, which has an interest in deceiving the public, that is to blame for this widespread confusion. The ownership of the capital wielded by and concentrated in the banks is certified by printed, and written certificates called shares, bonds, bills, receipts, etc. Not a single one of these certificates would be invalidated or altered if the banks were nationalized, i.e., if all the banks were amalgamated into a single state bank. Whoever owned fifteen rubles on a savings account would continue to be the owner of fifteen rubles after the nationalization of the banks; and whoever had fifteen million rubles would continue after the nationalization of the banks to have fifteen million rubles in the

form of shares, bonds, bills, commercial certificates and so on.«[93]

The nationalization of the banks (December 27, 1917) then also took place in this sense, which is shown by the fact that the industry remained in private ownership until the end of June 1918 and the entrepreneurs continued to hold the companies after the nationalization of the industry with "free rental and usage income".

According to the Bolsheviks, however, this system would not be ordinary state capitalism as we know it in Western Europe. *This system would be operated by the principles of the Paris Commune*, by the "revolutionary-democratic control" of company workers.

»*For control over the industry to be effectively carried out, it must be a **workers' control** with a workers' majority in all the leading bodies, and the management must give an account of its actions to all the authoritative workers' organizations.*«[94]

Accordingly, the first decree on workers' control (14 November 1917) provided that works councils were entrusted with the control of production, pricing,

---

[93] V. I. Lenin, The Impending Catastrophe and How to Combat It, collected works vol. 25
[94] V. I. Lenin, Speech Made at the First Petrograd Conference of Shop Committees May 31 (June 13), 191, collected works vol. 24. Highlighted by Lenin

purchasing of raw materials, and the financial policy of the operational unit. However, they were not allowed to interfere in the daily management of the operation or take their place, while "expropriation" was prohibited. These provisions applied to both public and private operational units. Considering that in the first decree, a national association of all control committees was immediately decided upon, the entire social life would be under the control of the workers. In the implementation of this decree, the leaders of economic life and the bureaucracy would be responsible downwards. They would not detach themselves from the masses but would be the executive organs of the workers. Under these circumstances, it would not be the manager of the factory who would be responsible for the production process, but the workers of the factory as a whole. There would be no individual responsibility but *a collective one*.

In practice, however, nothing has come of this decree. In other words, the cooperation of capital and labor on which it was based could not be introduced. The owners refused to work under this control – and sabotaged production ... or closed the factories. The bourgeoisie and its bureaucracy could not be put under the control of the workers.

»*The decree of the soviet power obliged the entrepreneurs to introduce workers' control in all areas. However, workers' control proved to be a half-measure and, therefore, not feasible. As a slogan, workers' control signified the growing and at the same time still insufficient power of the proletariat, that is, it was an expression of the movement's weakness, which has not yet been overcome.«*[95]

The Bolsheviks were thus faced with the choice of either abolishing workers' control or giving the workers the leadership of economic life by abandoning their state-capitalist plans. In reality, however, there was no choice: the working class was far too weak, ideologically and numerically to take over the leadership of economic life. There were only 2 million industrial workers with families, most of whom were still on the farm, compared with 120 million peasants (including families). And so, the Bolsheviks decided to abolish workers' control

From state capitalism under revolutionary-democratic control, only state capitalism remained!

---

[95] Larin und Kritzmann - Wirtschaftsleben und die wirtschaftlicher Aufbau in Sowjet-Russland, 1917 bis 1920 (Economic life and the economic construction in Soviet Russia, 1917 to 1920), Quoted by: A. Rosenberg, Geschichte des Bolschewismus (History of Bolshevism), p. 114

d. The destruction of workers' control by the Bolsheviks

Let us now proceed to show briefly the disempowerment of the working class by the Bolsheviks. To do this, we must focus on the relationship between the workers' councils and the trade union movement.

During the Kerensky period, there were two organizations of industrial workers side by side: the trade unions and the workers' councils. The workers' councils were the direct representatives of the workers in the factories; they themselves were also in the factory. The workers' councils were the real weapon of "direct action". A revolutionary core of workers from a factory called the entire workforce together for a general meeting, and there the position on the various issues was determined. The question was not: "Which party or union do you belong to?" It was completely indifferent. As an **operational unit,** the decisions were made, the class unit went beyond the fragmented spirit of the membership cards. The actions of the masses were thus taken out of the framework of the *leadership policies* of the various parties and unions and turned into *class politics*.

Of course, the trade unions and the social democrats were fierce opponents of the workers' councils. Only the Bolsheviks immediately supported them and organized them in a national context, because this lively activity of the masses would play an important role in the struggle for power for the Bolsheviks.

However, this only lasted until the masses had helped the Bolsheviks gain governmental power. They then strangled the workers' councils and went over to the trade-union front. As early as December 22, 1917, the Bolsheviks abolished workers' control of the Murmansk Railroad and a director appointed by the People's Commissariat of Transportation took its place. This was the sign for the further course of the revolution.

The Bolsheviks now set out to lead the revolution in "orderly" ways, and in order to enforce their leadership policy, it was above all important to get rid of the unpleasant workers' councils. They did this in the same way as the German Social Democracy, and the trade union movement would do a year later in Germany: They took them into the central apparatus of the trade union movement! (Legal works councils in Germany). It was a painful but short operation.

In January 1918 (when the Bolsheviks were in power for 2 months), they organized a joint congress of trade unions and works councils in order to achieve "cooperation" between the often-opposing movements. Because the Bolsheviks believed that the trade unions, together with the Supreme Economic Council, should take over the management of operational life, the trade unions had to be transformed into industrial unions on the one hand, and the works councils had to follow the central leadership on the other. The company organizations were to be the lowest "cells" of the industrial federations. This was the decision. However, this only happened after fierce resistance from the workers' councils. This was perfectly understandable. For every independent movement, the very principle of the life of the councils had been abandoned; all funds were placed in the hands of the central administrations. All independent funds in the factories (strike funds, support funds) were banned, which considerably restricted the workers' councils' own movement. In the opinion of the Bolsheviks, this self-movement was also completely superfluous, since, at the following trade union congress (20 April 1918), where they had the majority, they passed the following resolution

»Conflicts between workers and management must be immediately submitted to the central administration of the Federation of Trade Unions for decision. If the workers refuse to submit to the decisions of the trade union bodies, they must be

immediately expelled from the union and bear all the consequences resulting from it.«[96]

A second consequence of the joint meeting of unions and works councils (January 1918) was the *enormous growth* of the trade union movement. In addition to the inclusion of works councils, most of which were not unionized, a practically compulsory membership was now introduced, albeit not legally. A works meeting was called by the party cell of an operational unit, at which it was proposed to join the union jointly, which was then decided by a show of hands. If the operational unit had thus joined the union, all newly recruited workers would automatically be registered as members, with the contribution deducted from their wages. The growth of the trade union movement was therefore by no means the growth of the workers' "class consciousness", but membership of the union had become an "official obligation" (Tomski).

---

[96] Courier of the Ministers of Labor, 1918 No. 5/7, Organ of the People's Commissariat for Labor. Since there was compulsory membership in the union, expulsion also meant dismissal from the operational unit. As the trade unions were responsible for the distribution of food, the dismissal immediately meant the withholding of the food ration cards. Thus the dictatorship of the proletariat was made the dictatorship of the trade union bureaucracy as early as January 1918, which was then further confirmed in April.

»The workers accepted the withholding of contributions as an order from above, completely independent of their will.«[97]

However, the third and *most important* consequence of the joint meeting of unions and works councils (January 1918) was of a very different nature. *Only the workers' organizations recognized by the Central Council of Trade Unions were permitted by law.* Since membership of the official trade union was an *"official obligation"*, this meant nothing more or less than that the working class was deprived of the right to organize. One "was allowed", no, one *had to* be a member of the ally of the governmental party. In reality, the working class was not (and still is!) to be allowed to organize to defend its interests.

e. "The right to appoint and dismiss the members of the commune themselves placed all the officials under the control of the masses, they became the real executive organs of the masses..." (Marx - Civil war in France, p. 40)[98]

Since the working class was deprived of the right to organize already in the first period of the revolution

---

[97] Tomski, Prinzipien der Gewerkschaft (Principles of the union), p. 69

[98] The quotation cannot be found in the MEW. Probably the GIK quoted from an older edition in the MEW. See the fragment in MEW Vol. 17, p. 339

(the ruling party would represent its interests!), it is obvious that also the management of production by the workers, the responsibility "downwards" of all officials, was bound to be a charade. This is indeed the case. We have already pointed out the contradiction between the Supreme Economic Council and the factory organizations, for example, how the "Jivilov" starch factory was "nationalized", but the works council refused to hand over the factory to a representative of the Supreme Economic Council. The SEC introduced a system of inspectors to bring the Petrograd metal companies under its control, but serious conflicts arose between the inspectors and the works councils. It is also no coincidence that the Union of Workers' Representatives, which defended the "autonomy of the works councils", was created in the railway workshops because this is where the disempowerment of the workers' councils (Murmansk Railway) first began. However, the real struggle was fought out at the already mentioned trade union congress of 20 April 1918. The Bolsheviks proposed to abolish accountability "downwards" by proposing that the *individual responsibility* of the director be implemented from now on. This was decided. The director was thus no longer accountable to the workers of the factory, *but* to the "higher authorities", a responsibility which, of course, is only possible if he runs the factory "individually", without the workers. The workers were thus ousted from the management of the company, and "worker control" was reduced to checking that the director was complying with the labor law and collective agreements with the trade unions, which is the function of the statutory works councils in Germany. After the introduction of the New Economic Policy in March 1921, the trade unions were also ousted from production management, which in name was transferred to the Supreme Economic Council, but in reality to the tsarist bourgeoisie and its "spetzen" (specialists). That this situation still exists today is shown by the so-called **"Ramsin trial"** of 1930; all phrases about the dictatorship of the proletariat in Russia cannot hide the fact that the old bourgeoisie is responsible for production. These "red directors" are, of course, not responsible to the workers – because they are not appointed by them. In this context, we recall the resolution we published earlier, which was passed by the Central Committee of the CPR on September 7, 1929, <u>measures aimed at reorganizing the management of production and defining the dictatorial rights of factory management</u>.

Under the aspect of the "smashing of the state", the destruction of the old bureaucracy, the subjugation of all officials to the control of the masses, the Russian revolution is thus moving *further and further away from communism*. The separation of the masses from the management of production has become a fact, and thus the old situation of the bureaucratic rule has been restored in a new form. The Bolsheviks ultimately had to bow to the backwardness of the social structure in the agrarian country of Russia. They were forced *to "smash" the proletarian elements present in the Russian Revolution* and take over the old bureaucratic apparatus.

»**We took over the old machinery of state**, *and that was our misfortune. Very often, this machinery operates against us. In 1917, after we seized power, the government officials sabotaged us. This frightened us very much, and we pleaded:* **"Please come back."** *They all came back, but that was our misfortune.*«[99]

---

[99] V. I. Lenin, Fourth Congress of the Communist International, collected works vol. 33. p. 415f.
https://www.marxists.org/archive/lenin/works/1922/nov/04b.htm. Highlighted by GIC

The control of the operating life II

a. Control in state capitalism

If we now turn our attention to the control of operating life from an accounting point of view, it is obvious that the form of this control is closely related to the legal basis of the society. The type of control is therefore determined by the new ownership relations. When the means of production are transferred to state ownership, the regulation of production and distribution also becomes a state function, and control appears as top-down monitoring of compliance with state decrees. The state appoints an army of inspectors, accountants, etc. who are responsible for financial control. It is an unproductive apparatus that serves the state alone to ensure the appropriation of goods. To the extent that the state wants to make use of "workers' control" in this regard, it can only be a matter of monitoring compliance with the regulations laid down by the management. In state-capitalism, therefore, "worker control" can never go beyond the so-called "worker participation" in operational units.

Varga describes control under state capitalism as follows:

»*The functional area of the organizational-central management includes the control of the administration and financial management of state property, a problem that has caused particularly serious difficulties in Russia ... The frivolous handling of state property, of the expropriated assets of the bourgeoisie, arises above all from the greedy capitalist tendency of the entire society, whose morale was particularly undermined by the long war. However, a certain ambiguity about the new ownership structures also plays a role here. The proletarians who administer the expropriated operational units fall too easily into the belief that the units are their property, not that of the whole society. This makes a well-functioning control particularly important since it is also an excellent means of education ... The problem of control was solved very well in Hungary. (Emphasis by Varga.) Auditors, who used to serve the capitalists, were increased in number by training lawyers and secondary school teachers for this profession. As employees of the state, they were combined into a special section of the National Economic Council. The section was divided into professional groups so that the same auditors constantly controlled the companies of certain industries. The inspection covered not only money and material fees but also the correct use of labor, the investigation of the causes of poor performance or of the unfavorable result in general. The auditor in charge checked the company and accounts on the spot at certain intervals and wrote a report which not only revealed the errors but also contained proposals for reforms. The auditors themselves had no right of disposal in the companies they audited; they only submitted their reports to the responsible organizational author-*

ities. However, cooperation soon developed between the auditors, the production commissioner and the works council. The auditor's advice was often followed spontaneously. Also, a magazine called "Das Blatt der Revisoren" was founded, which was sent to all expropriated operations and did much to clarify the organizational questions of the management among the workers. The systematic control extended not only to the operations but also to the conduct of all People's Commissariats.«[100]

What Varga calls here the control of production is the confusion of two very different things. One is the control in the accounting sense - the control of the operational books; in other words, a question of income and expenditure. The other is technical control. It is a question of rationalizing production. The combination of these different functions is not a coincidence for state capitalism. They are an expression of the basis on which production stands: profitability. The control card system, stamp clocks, Taylor system, and assembly line are signposts of this rationalization, which is at the same time control, - but it is control of <u>superior power</u> over the work that is made to serve it. Control of production here means controlling the producers to see if they are profitable enough to produce enough surplus

---

[100] E. Varga, Die wirtschaftlichen Probleme der proletarischen Diktatur (The economic problems of the proletarian dictatorship), p. 67/68

for the economic command. Control has the character of domination over the producers.

b. Control under communism

In the association of free and equal producers based on the calculation of working hours, control is of a completely different nature, **because we are dealing with different legal relationships here**. The workers receive the buildings, machines, and raw materials from the community to produce new goods for the community. Each operational unit thus forms a collective legal entity which is responsible to the community for its management. Public accounting for all operations is a natural consequence of this.

As we have seen, the operational unit does not know "income and expenditure"; it can never work with "surpluses or deficits"; in other words, profitability does not exist under communism. Money does not exist. All transfers of goods are nothing more than a transfer by the giro office, while nobody can ever receive anything other than individual consumer goods. No one can have an "income" higher than the products he can take from consumption for the hours he works.

When we talk about the control of the economy under communism, we do not want to invent different committees to carry out this control. It is not that there will not be such bodies, but they fall outside the scope of theoretical research. We, therefore, only want to investigate what forms of control are directly embedded in the operating process of the economy. We mean the way in which operational life controls itself, without any "controller".

In the association of free and equal producers, the control of production is not carried out by persons or instances, but it is guided by the public registration of the factual course of operational life. That is, production is controlled by reproduction.

It must be considered that communism does not produce at random, but works according to a predetermined production plan, within which economic life will largely move. This production plan is no different from determining the scope of the various production areas. It, therefore, determines the amount of work that society will spend on the production of means of production, raw materials, food, entertainment, etc. These plans are not "invented" by economists, but are created from within society. Because consumption by all kinds of consumer organizations is directly linked to production, the companies know exactly how far they can meet the requirements for their products. If it turns out that the textile industry is not able to meet all the requirements, it will make proposals for above-average expansion when the next production plan is drawn up. In this way, the production plan "grows" out of the practice of life. However, once this plan has been adopted, the various operational organizations must also remain within this framework and must not exceed their production budgets. This is one of the **general rules** that the economy is run by.

In the general social accounting of the Giro Office, in this reduction mirror of the operational life, we already have an immediate overview of whether each sector is moving within the production plan. If each operational unit is part of the Giro Association, each individual operation is subject to this accounting control. If the entire production sector (e.g., the sugar industry as a whole) is affiliated, then the accounting control of the individual operations falls within the scope of this production association.

How does operational life control **itself**? It is the socially average production time that does so. In chapter 8, we have given an example of how the socially average production time can be determined. We saw there that not all operational units are equally productive, but that one is below and the other above the social average. If production shows that an operation's production time is well above the average, then the objective production itself indicates that an investigation of the causes is necessary.

It is also possible that societal production time itself has been incorrectly calculated. If it was too high, a larger number of hours is "transferred" to society in the accounts than was consumed in the operational units in the form of f, c, and l. However, where input and output power must always be the same, such a situation constitutes a miscalculation. The social average can also be calculated too low. In this case, this is reflected in the accounts, since the input quantity is greater than the output quantity. This is painful for the operational unit or the sector since the companies cannot reproduce themselves. This means that production comes to a standstill. So, this shows that the societal average production time is a relentless "controller", which is noticeable every time the operations break through it, voluntarily or involuntarily. Or, as one might say: production is controlled by reproduction. It is the laws of movement of the operational life **itself** that exercise control and immediately indicate a violation.

The control of public operations does not offer so many forms of automatic control since the product is "free" for consumption. There is usually no socially average production time, and the operational books usually do not indicate how much product has been "transferred".

These companies operate according to the formula f + c + l = "service". The reproductive process does not act as a control factor here either. In this case, social accounting can only check whether the "service" continues to be *within its production budget*, i.e., whether it does not exceed its consumption of f, c, and l. Whether the "service" is sufficiently productive cannot be determined here. Other means must, therefore, be used. For example, how many working hours are spent on one kilometer of tram transport, or a comparison of the "costs" of education in the different municipalities per capita, etc. But this kind of control does not fall within the scope of the investigations in this paper.

15.
The introduction of communism in agriculture

a. The development towards the production of commodities

It is a well-known saying that every new society is born from the womb of the old. Capitalism, in its rapid development, creates an ever more powerful and concentrated production apparatus, which on the one hand, reduces the number of the bourgeois who have control over the apparatus and, on the other hand, increases the army of proletarians immeasurably. This development also creates conditions that bring down capitalism. The necessary condition of this growth of the proletariat is increasingly intensive exploitation, while the insecurity of existence keeps pace with it. (See Marx, Wage Labor, and Capital.) Under these conditions, there is only one way out for the proletariat: communism.

If we look at the development of agriculture alongside this industrial development, we get a different picture. Notwithstanding all the prophecies that agriculture too must concentrate, that large agricultural syndicates will oust the small and middle peasant, little is to be noticed of this development. Not only the medium-sized farmer but also the small farmer has asserted himself, while there is no mention of development in a sense mentioned above. Yes, there have even been a sharp increase in small-scale farming.

In the eyes of the theorists of the state communism, this development is very disappointing. Work in the industry is taking on an increasingly social character, while that of the farmer, in their opinion, will remain isolated for some time to come. In industry, operational units are becoming more and more "mature" for communism, or what they understand by it. In agriculture, on the other hand, they do not want to "mature" for central state administration.

From the perspective of state communism, therefore, agriculture is and remains an obstacle to the introduction of communism. In our opinion, however, capitalism has brilliantly implemented the objective conditions for communism in agriculture as well. It only depends on how one sees things, whether one wants to put the administration of production in the hands of the central government offices, or whether one thinks it is carried out by the producers themselves.

To show that agriculture is already completely "ripe" for communism, we will give a brief overview of the situation of operational units as they are in

Western Europe, America, and Australia. (For further details we refer to our brochure: The development of the agricultural enterprise).[101] We will then see that agriculture has become thoroughly capitalist and that production is the same as in industry.

One of the characteristics of capitalist production is that it is a **"commodity"** production. "Commodities" are utensils that the producer produces not for himself but others, for society, and his work is, therefore, social work. In the social process of metabolism, all producers of commodities are therefore connected, they live in complete interdependence and thus, in reality, form a closed whole.

The old farming business knew the production of commodities only as a secondary matter. It was a world of its own in which almost everything it produced was self-consumption. The farmer was his own tailor, bricklayer, textile manufacturer, and food supplier. So, the farmer did not work for others, for society, but *for his own family circle*. The farmer brought very little to the market, which meant that he had very little money in his hands, but which at least gave him an "independent" existence.

---

[101] published in: De Niewe Weg – 1930, [https://www.aaap.be/Pages/Pamphlets-GIC-1930-De-Ontwikkeling-Van-Het-Boerenbedrijf.html].

The industrial production of commodities broke through this isolation. On the one hand, it knew how to spread a stream of cheap products over the earth, on the other hand, the effects of capitalism increased the rent, while the state also demanded ever-higher taxes. It is not our task here to follow the process of breaking up the closed domestic economy. (See R. Luxemburg, The Accumulation of Capital.) We only want to ascertain the result, which is clearly visible to everyone. *The peasant farm needed more and more money to meet its obligations.* But it can only receive money by acting as a producer of commodities, by putting more product on the market. There were two ways to do this. Either the farmer himself had to consume less for the same productivity, or he had to increase the productivity of his work. But to consume even less, as a farmer of old grist and grain, is one of the impossible. Increasing productivity seemed to be the only solution.

This is the point where economists have been mistaken in their speculations about the future. *They assumed the same development for the agricultural enterprise as for the industry.* In industry, productivity was always increasing, through the merging of capital, through new, more productive machines, which could only be used in huge enterprises. In this respect, they thought that the same concentration process should take place in agriculture. This meant that the small and medium-sized farmers would have to disappear in the main, while the agricultural consortium would play the decisive role in agriculture. The small and medium-sized farmers would all be made wage laborers of the share capital in agriculture.

So, our economists were very wrong in this respect. It is remarkable, however, that industrial development, which was to bring about concentration in agriculture, itself prepared the ground for a very different development of agriculture. It was, in particular, the **motor**, **artificial fertilizers,** and **agronomy** that managed to increase the productivity of work enormously without leading to this great concentration of capital. Modern fertilization made the nature of the soil less important, the yield per hectare grew enormously, which enabled the farmer to bring many more goods to the market than in the past, while **modern transport** could provide an all-round service.

At the same time, as the yield per hectare increased, a phenomenon of enormous importance took place. As soon as production is based on science, the phenomenon of <u>specialization</u> appears with compelling force. "The specialist is a caveman, he sees only a small strip of light from space, but he sees it very sharply," Multatuli says somewhere. So, we can see how the farmer sets himself up to supply only a certain product, but in order to achieve the highest possible level of quality, which is possible with the current state of science and technology – and his financial resources. According to this specialization, he then sets up his business, i.e., he procures the tools he needs for the special product.

This is the current state of agriculture in Western Europe, America, and Australia. *The farmer has thus become a producer of goods in the full sense of the word!* He no longer puts his surplus on the market when he has provided for his own needs, but his whole product. He creates that which he does not consume himself, and he consumes precisely that which he does not produce himself. So, he does not work for his family circle, but for others, for society, and so his work is now social work. The closed domestic economy has been destroyed by specialization. The peasant business has gone over to "industrial production".

Although the farmer may have remained the "owner" of his land, his position has deteriorated enormously. Certainly, he can do good business when the economy is favorable, but he is now completely dependent on the vicissitudes of the market. His uncertainty has kept pace with his specialization. Of course, this did not remain hidden from the farmers, and they tried to avoid the fatal tendencies of their specialization. To this end, they founded farmers' cooperatives, which gave them better control over prices and also enabled them to procure machines for working the fields and processing the harvest collectively. As a result, the entire agricultural enterprise is highly concentrated, even though there is no question of an industrial concentration of the farms.

b. The significance of this development for the proletarian revolution

The course of development outlined above prevents the formation of a large number of land proletariat. Even if it is still much larger than the number of owning peasants, it is still far from being in the same proportion as the urban population. Besides, the class antagonisms in the countryside do not come to the fore so much, precisely because the small farmer himself works with his family members. If ownership in the cities has led to pure parasitism, this is not the case with the small and medium-sized farm. This makes a communist revolution much more difficult in the countryside than in the cities.

But the conditions are not as hopeless as they appear at first sight. Certainly, there are a relatively large number of "owners" in the countryside, but they know very well that they are not much more than the toiling agents of bond capital. At the same time, the burden of uncertainty weighs heavily on them. No doubt, it remains true that the "owning" peasant will never be a champion of communism, but he rejoices in the struggle of the working class against capital. *What* the attitude of the small and middle peasant will be in a proletarian revolution cannot be said with certainty. The only way to find out is to examine the attitude of the peasants in the proletarian movements in Germany in 1918-1923. We do not have more experience material yet. We will come back to this later.

The fact that the peasant has become a commodity producer is of the utmost importance to the proletarian revolution. This is still too much overlooked within the working class. As a result, we hear all kinds of reservations about the opposition that the peasants would place against a victorious working class, which in reality no longer makes sense. They are still based on a situation as it *was* in the past. For example, it is constantly pointed out that the working classes should convince the peasant because the cities depend on the countryside for their food supply.

This is undoubtedly true. But the farmers today are also dependent on the city. If the farmers do not deliver their product to the cities, then they are as much at the mercy of hunger as the working class, paradoxical as this may sound. Despite everything, the peasant *must* sell his product. Otherwise, he would not be able to feed himself because he only produces what he does not consume and has to consume what he does not produce himself. One also often hears the remark that the farmer would rather feed his product to the animals than supply it to the revolutionary working class. This too is a misunderstanding, which is due to the outdated view of the closed domestic economy. The cattle farmer has only cattle (apart from the by-products) and nothing else. The arable farmer may have grain but no livestock, the chicken farmer several hundred chickens, the vegetable farmer only a certain number of vegetables. They are all specialists.

Besides, one also hears the fear that the farmer will refuse to cultivate his land further, i.e., that he will try to return to the closed domestic economy. But he cannot do that either. Even a farmer cannot go back a century and make everything necessary himself, because he has neither the necessary skills nor the necessary tools. Once the socialization of work has been completed, no one can escape it any longer, and a return has become impossible. No matter how one turns or twists the matter, the peasants are on the social ship and must go with it.

c. The agricultural proletariat and the small and middle peasants in the German Revolution

Let us now take a closer look at the attitude of the peasants in the German Revolution. For this purpose, however, it is necessary to describe briefly the general situation in November 1918.

When the imperial violence collapsed in Germany in November 1918, it was certainly *not* through the proletarian revolutionary activity of the masses. The war front collapsed, the soldiers deserted by the thousands. In this situation, the German navy wanted to try one last big effort by a persistent blow against the English. The sailors thought, rightly or wrongly, that they would all die in the process, and this became the instruction for mass denial of service on the warships. Once on this course, the sailors *had to* continue, because otherwise the mutinous ships would have been shot to the ground by the "faithful" troops. They, therefore, raised the red flag, which led to the revolt of the other warships. Herewith the redemptive act was done. The sailors would have to go on now if they did not want to be shot by the land army. With iron necessity, one deed developed from the other. So, they marched to Hamburg to call for help from the workers. How would they be received here? Would they be beaten back?

There was no talk of any resistance. Hundreds of thousands of workers declared their solidarity with the sailors, and the revolutionary activity was expressed in the workers' and soldiers' councils. Thus, began the triumphal procession of the revolution throughout Germany. And this was the strange thing. Although the military censorship had all reports of the Russian revolution of 1917 under its control, although no propaganda was made for the idea of councils, and although the Russian structure of councils was completely unknown to the German workers, a whole network of councils had spread over Germany in the space of a few days.

The civil war that now followed was under the sign of socialism. On the one hand, social-democracy, which saw socialism as a simple continuation of the concentration process of capitalism, with the legal nationalization of big industry, and which had to destroy the councils as the embodiment of the self-activity of the masses. On the other hand, the newborn communism, which considered "nationalization" only attainable by illegal means. The *goal was the same*, but the path was not.

Although the occupation of the factories by the proletariat was generally carried out throughout the entire revolutionary period, nowhere did it come to "occupation in the name of society". The factories always remained the property of the old owners, even here and there under the very primitive control of the workers. The fact that it did not go further is due to the lack of self-confidence of the German working class. The workers listened to the German counter-revolution, which under the leadership of Social Democracy wanted to prevent the workers from "arbitrary" expropriation. On the other hand, the revolutionary part of the working class that wanted to move to direct expropriation was still far too weak. The proletariat itself seemed to be divided on the questions of communism, and consequently, the revolution was very weak. The revolutionary working class had to join all its forces to defend itself against counterrevolution and could not yet think of expropriating its owners. It goes without saying that this is why the large middle classes in society, who are forced to defect to the victor in the revolution, were driven into counterrevolution by themselves.

This applies first and foremost to the peasants. If communism was so weak in the German proletariat, how much weaker should it be among the peasants? In fact, we see that the peasants were not an essential factor in the revolution. There was no independent organization with its own position, with the exception of Bavaria, when the dictatorship of the proletariat was declared there. Here the peasants had to speak out, and the same phenomenon was evident as with the proletariat, they did not appear as a closed unit. One part of the peasants choose the side of the revolution; another part opposed it. (As far as we know, there is no data on the character of the peasant farms which took the side of the revolution. There is also a lack of more precise numerical ratios).

Except in Bavaria, the farmers hardly took part in the revolution. There was no talk of direct support, and the general mood was clearly antipathetic. The slogan: "The land to the farmers" made no sense in Germany, because small and medium-sized operational units are strongly represented. Although there is still a great deal of large land ownership in Germany, the peasants have shown no willingness to divide these goods. While the primitive slogan "The land to the farmers" could unleash such enormous psychological forces in backward agricultural areas, this slogan proved to be without influence in Germany with its large agricultural enterprises based on scientific agriculture.

The explanation for this must lie in the nature of the Western conglomerate, which functions directly as an "industry". The large grain estates are worked with modern machines, and the grain is stored in large barns. In the cattle breeding areas, there are extensive pastures with stabling facilities for hundreds of cows, while the milk is prepared in the company's own dairies. The large potato fields in the north are entirely specialized in this crop, and the liquor factory is grafted directly onto them. The situation is similar in the province of Saxony, where everything is specialized in sugar beet cultivation for the affiliated sugar factories in Magdeburg etc.

In these conditions, the slogan: "The land to the farmers" in the sense of the land division according to the Russian model cannot find a breeding ground. The agricultural workers would not know what to do with the land. In the cattle area, they could, however, get a piece of land and a few cows, but because their dwellings are not furnished as a farm, they would not be able to run the business of cattle breeders or dairy farmers after all. On top of that, they lack the tools to exploit their property.

These conditions apply to the whole of German large-scale land ownership, and we can, therefore, say that the highly developed state of agriculture prevents land from being divided up. The workers who create there are faced with the same problem as the industrial workers, with the "takeover as a whole in the name of society". But the agrarian proletariat did not even come to the problem in the German revolution. The agrarian relations of production determine that thousands of proletarians do not find their conditions of solidarity within a small area, which makes it difficult to establish a united front of struggle. The German agricultural proletariat did not or hardly ever form councils and played no role in the German revolution.

Peculiar was the attitude of the so-called "semi-proletariat" in the countryside. In particular, in Germany, there is a lot of industry in the countryside, a phenomenon which is also becoming more and more prevalent in the Netherlands. This may coincide with cheaper labor, as well as with lower land prices and other burdens. Because the workers needed are recruited from the peasant population of the surrounding area, and because they work a fairly large piece of land in their free time, they occupy an intermediate position, which we call semi-proletariat. The character of their agriculture is that of a closed domestic economy. What comes from them to the market is not important.

The peculiar thing now is that this semi-proletariat was a force that stopped at nothing in the revolution. Several times they went forward in the movement; they went on strike and marched to the surrounding towns to broaden the basis of the struggle. Thuringia is a telling example of this. But these workers also did an excellent job of supplying the cities with food. At the beginning of the revolution, when the councils still held power, the peasants held on to the food in order to raise prices. The councils in the city then contacted the councils of the factories in the countryside, and the semi-proletarians, who were completely familiar with the situation there, *forced* the peasants to deliver their product at fixed prices. (Hamburg.)

In summary, we can say that, in general, neither the German agricultural proletariat nor the German peasant participated in the revolution. Even though the agricultural proletariat may have had communist reflections, they were still extraordinarily weak, which meant that they could not yet express them. It seems that the peasants adopt a wait-and-see attitude in a proletarian revolution. This will generally be determined by the force of the revolution and by whether the large agricultural operational units intervene in communist production.

16.
The economic dictatorship of the proletariat

Finally, we must say a few words about the dictatorship of the proletariat. This dictatorship is self-evident to us and does not really need special treatment, because the introduction of communist economic life *is* nothing other than the dictatorship of the proletariat. The introduction of communist economic life means nothing other than the abolition of wage labor, the implementation of the *equal right* of all producers to the social stocks. It means the abolition of all privileges of certain classes. Communist business life does not give anyone the right to enrich himself at the expense of labor. Those who do not work will not eat. The introduction of these principles is by no means "democratic". The working class carries them out in the most intense and bloody struggle. There is no question of "democracy" in the sense of cooperation between the classes as we know it at present in the parliamentary and trade union system.

But if we look at this dictatorship of the proletariat from the perspective of the transformation of social relations, from the perspective of the mutual relations of the people, then this dictatorship is the real conquest of democracy. Communism means nothing other than that humanity is advancing to a higher cultural level, since all social functions are placed under the direct direction and control of all workers, thus taking their fate into their own hands. This means that democracy has become the life principle of society. Therefore, a substantial democracy rooted in the administration of social life by the working masses corresponds exactly to the dictatorship of the proletariat.

Once again, it was up to Russia to turn this dictatorship into a caricature, in that the dictatorship of the Bolshevik Party was declared the dictatorship of the proletarian **class**. This closed the door to real proletarian democracy, the administration, and management of social life by the masses themselves. The dictatorship of a party is the form in which the dictatorship of the proletariat is actually prevented.

In addition to the social significance of the dictatorship, we also consider its economic content. In the economic sphere, the dictatorship works by making the new social rules to which operational life is subject generally applicable. The workers can bring *all* social activities themselves into communist operational life by accepting its principles, by carrying out production for the community under the responsibility of the community. All together carry out communist production.

It is obvious that various parts of the agricule will not directly comply with the rules of communist operational life, i.e., will not join the communist community. It is also probable that some workers will interpret communism in such a way that they will want to run the operational units independently, but not under the control of society. Instead of the private capitalist of the past, the business organization acts as a "capitalist".

Here the economic dictatorship has the special function of organizing the economy according to the general rules, in which the social accounting in the general giro office fulfills an important function. In social accounting, we find the recording of the flow of goods within the communist economy. This means nothing else than that those who are not members of the social accounting cannot receive raw materials. Because under communism, nothing is "bought" or "sold". Producers can only receive goods and raw materials from the community for further distribution or processing. However, those who do not want to include their work in the socially regulated work process exclude themselves from the communist community. In this way, the economic dictatorship leads to the *self-organization* of all producers, regardless of whether they are small or large scale operational units, whether they are industrial or agricultural. In fact, this dictatorship is immediately lifted as soon as the producers include their work in the social process and work according to the principles of abolishing wage labor and social control. It is, therefore, a dictatorship which "dies" of its own accord as soon as the whole of social life is placed on the new foundations of the abolition of wage labor. It is also a dictatorship which is not carried out by bayonet, but by the economic laws of movement of communism. It is not "the state" that carries out this economic dictatorship, but something more powerful than the state: the laws of economic movement.

17.
Final considerations

a. The progress in our class goal

In the previous chapters, we have briefly presented the fundamental principles of communist operational life. We have shown what free and equal producers are, what the abolition of money, the market, and wage labor means; we have seen what it means that communist enterprises know no real income and expenditure, no assets and no debts, and we have also shown the new legal relations for the building of communism.

So, we as workers have grown very much in self-confidence. Because if you look at things more closely, it becomes clear that the workers *themselves* never came up with a communist objective. So far, the working class has followed in the wake of intellectuals and officials who view communism from *their* own interests. Although they speak of the social revolution that will create new social relations (these are immediately new legal relations), however, they stubbornly refuse to develop these new legal relations further.

This is perfectly understandable. In their train of thought, they will be the ones who will have to take over the actual management of operational life.

From their point of view, therefore, a closer look at the laws of movement of communism, the abolition of wage labor, is completely unnecessary, even harmful.

It is no coincidence, then, that these "fundamental principles", which look at communism precisely from the point of view of the wage laborer, were born from the heart of the proletariat. As ordinary proletarians who normally do the dirty work, we have wondered how the interests of *our* class are safeguarded. Therefore, we have not been content with the formula that the social revolution creates new legal relations, but we will determine the content of these new relations *ourselves*. It goes without saying that the socialism of intellectuals will contradict these views.

b. From the money account to the working time account

The extent to which the working class will be able to break this resistance cannot be further investigated at present, which is why we leave this question alone. We must, however, say a word about the transition from the capitalist money calculation to the working time calculation.

How is money abolished? How is operational life transferred to the working time calculation?

To shed light on this issue, we shall apply the usual method, examining what the practice of capitalism has already taught us in this area. So, we will not "invent" a solution, but we will ask a question to history. In fact, we have already received practical lessons, since several countries began to introduce a new unit of account after the war.

As is well known, most countries experienced enormous inflation after the war. Russia and the European states obtained the necessary state money by having more and more paper money printed, as a result of which the value of the money decreased from day to day, i.e., the prices of the products increased every day. The whole economic life was more and more disturbed, and finally, the money had become completely worthless in some countries. In this situation, it was necessary to stabilize the value of money, which was done by introducing a new unit of account. For example, Russia got its Chernovtsy instead of the old ruble, Germany got its Goldmark, Austria its Schilling, Belgium its Belga.

Above all, Germany gave visual instruction on the introduction of a new unit of account. Here it was simply stated that from a certain date on, a trillion paper stamps (million times million) would be equal to the value of a gold mark. Social life adapted wonderfully to this "largest and most difficult financial operation ever attempted" (The New Statesman).

Certainly, this expropriated several thousand small owners, but big business was saved, and the economy was able to get back on track with its calculations.

In the case of a proletarian revolution, the same phenomena will undoubtedly be repeated. In its first period of existence, the proletarian dictatorship needs an enormous amount of money, which it has to obtain through the banknote press, like the capitalist states from 1918 to 1923. For the proletariat, however, this is not a means of abolishing money in order to enter into a moneyless society, as the Russians believed. Surely a Council government would want to avoid as far as possible the scourge of inflation, which hits the working class above all. But there is no choice. Whatever the course of the revolution, whether it leads to state communism or the association of free and equal producers, whether a party succeeds in usurping the dictatorship or that the proletarian class as such exercises it through its councils, in any case, inflation will occur.

As a result, the already disrupted operational life would come to a complete standstill, so that the working class is faced with the question of "stabilization", with the introduction of a new unit of account. If the working class lacks the strength to implement communism, a new currency, a new kind of money will be created. When the workers have so much control over the operational units that they can abolish wage labor, then they will move towards the abolition of money by introducing working hours as the unit of account. The conversion of money into working hours will then be done in the same way as in the past the conversion of paper marks into gold marks. It is a simple operation that anyone can perform and that all operational organizations can use to calculate the production time for their product.

c. The "key number"

Of course, it is difficult to determine exactly how many working hours correspond to one guilder, for example. We cannot arbitrarily assume that one guilder corresponds to one hour or two hours of work. That is why this figure must be calculated as accurately as possible. It is, therefore, necessary to check how long the production time for a particular product has lasted. The best industries for such calculations are those that supply a mass product such as coal, electricity, iron, or potassium. From the operational books, it is possible to see how many **tons of product** were produced in a given time, what the

<u>actual cost price</u> was. From this, if one omits interest on capital, etc., it is possible to determine how many **working hours** were used. From this data, the monetary value can be calculated for an iron hour, coal hour, or potash hour, after which the average of all these industries can be taken as a provisional general average.

If this average turns out to be 0.80 Dollar 1 working hour, then each operational unit can calculate a provisional production time for its product. It is now possible in all operational units to convert the total stock into working hours by multiplying all monetary amounts expressed in marks by $1^1/_4$. This figure is the key figure.

The calculation of a shoe company would therefore read

f = used tools, buildings, etc. Mark 1,000 = 1,250 working hours

c = leather and so on Mark 49,000 = 61,250 working hours

l = hours worked 62,500

f + c + l are 125,000 working hours

According to our previous assumption, 40,000 pairs of shoes were produced, so that the average production time is 3.125 hours per pair of shoes.

We are not saying that the key number or "index" *has to* be found in the above-mentioned way, we are just saying that it can be found in this way. There are many ways to reach the goal. It is not possible to calculate the first key number exactly. We can only try to estimate it as accurately as possible. As soon as the calculation has been generally implemented, the actual production times are displayed very quickly.[102]

d. Utopism

With this, we want to conclude our study for the time being. Certainly, the subject is not exhausted, but we do not want more than to put the discussion about communism on a new basis in order to achieve a common proletarian goal in the labor movement. To deepen this discussion, we pointed out the utopian character of the constructions of socialism as we know them in Cole's Guild Socialism and the socialization reports. One does projects on

---

[102] There was a similar problem in Russia. During the so-called "war communism", companies no longer calculated with money. When money of stable value was reintroduced in 1921, companies did not know how much their product actually cost. They therefore set prices arbitrarily, usually based on pre-war prices. Thus, in 1922-23 we see an average wholesale price of 122 (22% higher than in 1913), but these prices soon proved to be completely wrong. They rose very quickly, averaging 170 the following year.

how to organize the different industries, how to abolish the opposition between producer and consumer through certain commissions and councils, through which organs the power of the state should be tamed, etc. If such an author gets into a jam with his fantastic somersaults, a difficulty arises in his theoretical considerations regarding the cooperation of the different industries - the solution is soon there. A new commission or a special council will be "brought into being". This is especially true of Cole's Guild Socialism, which makes that all these considerations are just nonsense.

The organizational structure of the production and distribution apparatus is functionally linked to the economic laws according to which it moves. All considerations of this construction are utopian stuff, as long as the economic categories that are the basis of this construction are not represented. It is utopia and distracts attention from the fundamental problems.

In our considerations, we have consistently adhered to the economic laws. As far as the organizational structure was concerned, we only referred to the operational organizations and cooperatives. We were entitled to do so because history has already indicated these forms. We have treated the organization of farmers with the greatest restraint precisely because Western Europe has very little experience in this area. That is why we only showed how capitalism has developed the conditions for calculating the socially average production time of products.

We did not go into too much detail in further organizational development. How the organizations of the operational units connect, the organs they create for the "smooth course" of production, these are all problems which are determined by the special conditions and, therefore, cannot be examined in advance.

e. Summary

Let us summarize our considerations briefly, then the following picture emerges:

The basis of these studies is the empirical fact that when power is taken over, the means of production are in the hands of the operational organizations. The strength of the communist mentality, which again is related to the clear understanding of what to do with the means of production, will determine whether they will *keep them*. But if they do not keep them, they will go to state communism, which cannot abolish wage labor. If they keep the means of production, then they cannot order production and consumption in any other way than based on the socially average production time, with the abolition of money. It is also possible that there are such strong syndicalist tendencies that the workers want to try to take the operational units into their own management, to regard them as their "property", in order to distribute the "full proceeds of labor" among the employees of the unit. This kind of "communism" cannot abolish money and leads from guild socialism to state capitalism. In our view, the main focus of the proletarian revolution is to establish an exact relationship between the producer and the product, and this is only possible if the calculation of working hours in production and consumption is carried out on all sides. It is the highest demand the proletariat can make –, but at the same time, it is also the lowest. It is a decisive question of power which the proletariat has to fight through on its own, because under no circumstances can it count on the help of other social groups.

The *assertion* of the operational organizations thus refers to independent administration and management. This is, therefore, the only basis on which the calculation of working hours can really be carried out. A veritable stream of literature from America, England, and Germany provides evidence of how the calculation of the average social production time is prepared by capitalism. (The modern cost accounting). In communism, the calculation of $(f + c) + l$ goes just as well as now, only with a different unit of account; in this respect, the old capitalist society carries the new communist one in its womb. In communism, the accounting between operational units will go through the general social accounting, through the giro office – just as in capitalism. Here too, capitalism gives birth to the new order. The consolidation of operational units is a process that is still taking place today. Future grouping will probably be different because it is based on different criteria. The operational units, which we called the GSW type, the so-called "public" operations that exist today but function as instruments of the class state, will be modeled as communist branches of industry. They will be detached from the state and integrated into society. There will still be a state because the bourgeoisie has been defeated but has not yet disappeared. But the state will then be clearly visible to all as the organ of repression of counterrevolution, – but it will have to do nothing with production or distribution. Here, at the same time, the conditions will be present under which the state can actually "die".

Tearing away the public operational units from the state, their insertion into the economic whole requires the identification of that part of the social product, which still needs to be distributed individually, for which we found the factor of individual consumption (FIC).

If we oppose this to state communism or state capitalism here, it becomes immediately clear that in the latter, there can be no exact relationship between the producer and the social product. The worker is a state worker and receives his wage from the state. The collective agreements with the unions determine the amount of this wage. The administration of production is in the hands of the state bureaucracy, whereby the producers are guaranteed "workers participation" by the unions. Democracy thus becomes the *cover* behind which the real control of millions is hidden, exactly as in capitalism.

f. Centralism - Federalism

So, if we reject the notion that industry is centrally managed and controlled, that does not mean that we will be operating on a purely federal basis. Where the administration and control of production is the responsibility of the masses, there are undoubtedly strong federalist tendencies. From general social accounting, however, economic life is an uninterrupted whole, and we have a center from which production, although not controlled and managed, can undoubtedly be monitored. The fact that all transformations of human energies in operational life are recorded in one organism represents the highest summary of economic events. Whether we want to call it federalist or centralist depends only on which side we see the same thing from. It is both one and the other, which is why these terms have lost their meaning for the production process as a totality. The contrast between centralism and federalism was abolished in a higher entity; the organism of production became an organic unity.

Appendix

The following notes, we have made during our research on the development in Russia. We print them here because the reader could benefit from them.

The course of nationalization in Soviet Russia from November 1917 to 1921

November 7, 1917

The Bolsheviks take over the government. Piatakov becomes director of the State Bank.

14 November 1917

Decree on Workers' Control. The workers are not allowed to expropriate companies on their own initiative and not to interfere with the daily management of the company.

30 November 1917

Creation of the Council for Labor and Distribution (STO).

5 December 1917

Creation of the Supreme Economic Council (OVWR). Consisting of trade unions, works committees, experts and members of the government. The Sergief Mining Company and the Putilov Works are nationalized.

19 December 1917

International Sleeping Car-Company nationalized

27 December 1917

Decree on the nationalization of banks.

3 January 1918

Decree on the nationalization of enterprises. The OVWR can only nationalize them and that is:

1st. If they are of great importance to the state.

2nd. If the entrepreneurs do not want to comply with the measures for workers' control.

3rd. If the entrepreneurs close or leave the enterprise.

26 January 1918

Nationalization of water transport and grain stores.

28 January 1918

Decree canceling the national debt.

17 February 1918

Nationalization of the electricity companies.

18 February 1918

Congress of works councils and trade unions. It is decided that the works council movement will be subordinated to the unions.

27 February 1918

Nationalization of the Chaudoir Company.

2 March 1918

Peace of Brest-Litovsk.

3 March 1918

Nationalization of a mining company in Novorossisk and a steel mill in Yuzovka.

April 1918

State monopoly for matches, coffee, spices, and yarn.

April 23, 1918

State monopoly on foreign trade.

May 1918

1st Congress of Economic Councils. It is emphasized once again that "arbitrary" nationalization is prohibited. The OVWR manages the sugar industry.

June 1918

The OVWR administers the oil industry.

June 28, 1918

Decree on the nationalization of all companies with more than 1 million share capital. Besides, all **mines, railways, rubber** and **pulp mills.** This decree is in contrast to the 1st Congress of Economic Councils, which wanted to implement the incorporation into the state very slowly. The nationalization was, however, for the time being purely formal, as the owners kept the companies in "free lease and usufruct". For the first time, the specialists were called "servants of the Republic". They remained in their old positions and on their old salaries.

July 1918

Start of the counterrevolution. In fact, the counterrevolution began a little earlier. 29 May - uprising of Czechoslovakians in the Urals. 30 May - State of siege in Moscow. 6 July - Armed uprising of the left [social] revolutionaries in Moscow. 29 July - Start of Allied intervention in Murmansk. 30 July - Czechoslovakians conquer Kazan. September 5: Assassination attempt on Lenin. Start of the Red Terror.

21 August 1918

Private trade is suspended. Narcomprod has to take care of the procurement and distribution of consumer goods. Thus, this function is taken away from the OVWR, which is only responsible for the means of production and raw materials.

December 1918

The industry is almost completely nationalized.

October 1919

Number of companies in the consumer industry/number of workers: 6675 / 1,185,000

October 1919

nationalized 2,522 / 750,000; April 1920 - nationalized 4,141 / 983,000

20 November 1920

The OVWR nationalizes all enterprises with mechanical power sources with five or more workers and all enterprises without mechanical power sources with ten or more workers.

The course of the peasant movement in Russia from 1917 to 1921

The course of the peasant movement until March 1921 can be divided into four periods. These are:

the 1st Peasant Revolution, the 2nd Peasant Revolution, attempts to socialize agriculture through soviets and kolkhozes, and finally the state production plan. In the First Peasant Revolution, the peasants divided the land, with the poorest peasants taking the least. This was a completely "natural" distribution since the poor farmer had no tools to cultivate the land. Those who had horses, plows, and storage facilities could work more land. However, it turned out that the better-off farmers did not want to give grain to the government for the food supply in the cities. They hid the supplies. Therefore, the Bolsheviks went to intervene through the poor farmers. They formed the Village Poverty Committees, which had to confiscate the supplies. This was the beginning of the Second Peasant Revolution. The result was that the yield of agriculture declined even further. Farms yielded nothing at all. The village poverty committees also failed to supply grain. Under these circumstances, the village poverty committees were abolished after a short time and the focus shifted back to the "middle farmers". This marks the beginning of the third period. However, the attempts of socialization by collective farms and soviets failed completely. Ossinski, therefore, proposed a new farmers' policy, according to which all farms were to be run under central state control and according to state regulations. In three months, this led to serious peasant uprisings and thus to a complete fiasco of the state production plan.

Here are some details relating to the farmers' movement.

First Peasant Revolution

November 7, 1917

The Bolsheviks take over the government.

9 November 1917

Decree on the Expropriation of Landowners. This was the basis for the so-called "Smychka", the alliance of the peasants with the proletariat of the cities. "The peasants divide the land, not the poorest but the wealthiest peasants receiving the larger share."

February 19, 1918

Land constitution. The Social Revolutionaries' program is taken over.

May 9, 1918

Narcomprod (Food Supply Council) **is given the right to confiscate grain stocks from the peasants,** which it does as early as May 13.

13 May 1918

The grain monopoly is introduced.

Second Peasant Revolution

11 June 1918

Decree on the organization of village poverty committees. They are given the right by state authorities and are allowed to confiscate the stocks of the wealthy peasants to deliver them to the towns in exchange for industrial products. They can also expropriate the rich farmers and distribute the means of production. This leads to further destruction of productive farms.

August 21, 1918

Private trade is completely forbidden.

December 1918

The village poverty committees are abolished. They have not achieved their goal, because, like the rich farmers, they have not delivered grain to the city. Therefore, from now on the grain must be confiscated with "75 men and 3 machine guns".

Fruitless experiments with sovkhozes and kolkhozes

March 1919

8th Party Congress. The policy of village poverty is abandoned. The fellow farmer becomes the "central figure" (Lenin).

From 1919 to 1920

The attempts at socialization through kolkhozes and collectives. In 1919, 2,500 farms were converted into Soviet operational units (sovkhozes). However, they did not deliver much, as they used almost all of their income themselves.

December 1919

The counter-revolutionary armies are finally defeated.

January 26, 1920

The Entente lifted the blockade.

February 1920

Trotsky demands that a tax of nature replace the confiscations. Rejected because it was seen as a concession to the kulaks (wealthy peasants) and a step back to free trade.

State production plan for agriculture

November 1920

The 8th Soviet Congress approves the general socialization of agriculture. The 18 million peasant farms are placed under a central administration that draws up a production plan that determines what, how much, and where to sow. Ossinsky was the driving force behind this plan because, in his opinion, the socialist construction of agriculture was impossible on the path of the sovkhozes and kolkhozes. Ossinsky issued the corresponding decree. The plan ended in a complete fiasco. The peasants reacted with heavy uprisings, which culminated in the Kronstadt rebellion.

21 March 1921

Introduction of the New Economic Policy (NÖP)

Some notes on freight transport

7 May 1918

Start of the "Communist Saturdays".

8 August 1918

Decree on the exchange of goods with farmers. At least 85% of the industrial products supplied must be paid for in agricultural products, while a maximum of 15% is allowed in cash. The prices are fixed.

January 1919

Abolition of letter postage.

20 February 1919

Decree on the transport of goods between state enterprises without bank transfer or settlement.

8 March 1919

8th Party Congress - the population is forced to join consumer cooperatives. Until now, there were two cooperatives in each city: one bourgeois and one proletarian. These were now merged into "consumer cooperatives," which were combined in Centrosojus (Central Cooperative) and led by Narcomprod.

1 June 1919

Introduction of free rail freight transport.

Literature

H. Block, Die Marxsche Geldtheorie (The Marxist Theory of Money), Jena 1926

G. D. H. Cole, Selbstverwaltung in der Industrie (Self-government in industry), Berlin, 1921.

H. Cunow, Die Marxsche Geschichts-, Gesellschafts- und Staatstheorie (Marxist theory of history, society and the state; principles of Marxist sociology), Band 1, Vorwärts, Berlin, 1920.

M. Dobb, Russian economic development, G. Routledge, London, 1929.

S. Faure, Het Universele Geluk (My Communism: Universal Happiness), Roode Bibliotheek, Zandvoort, 1927.

Groep van Int. Communisten, Ontwikkelingslijnen in het boerenbedrijf (Lines of development in farming). – In: De Nieuwe Weg, 1930.

A. Goldschmidt, Wirtschaftorganisation Sowjet-Russlands (Economic Organization in Soviet Russia), Rohwoltverlag, Berlin, 1920.

R. Hilferding, Das Finanzkapital (Finance Capital), 2. Auflage, Wien 1920

E. Horn, Die ökonomische Grenzen der Gemeinwirtschaft (The economic limits of the communal economy), Halberstadt, 1928.

K. Kautsky, Die proletarische Revolution und ihr Programm (The proletarian revolution and its program), Dietz, 1922.

O. Leichter, Die Wirtschaftsrechnung in der sozialistischen Gemeinschaft (The economic account in the socialist community), Wien, 1923.

W. I. Lenin,
State and Revolution, collected works vol. 25,
www.marxists.org/archive/lenin/works/1917/staterev/

The Immediate Tasks of the Soviet Government, collected works vol. 27,
www.marxists.org/archive/lenin/works/1918/mar/x03.htm

The Impending Catastrophe and How to Combat It, collected works vol. 25,
www.marxists.org/archive/lenin/works/1917/ichtci/index.htm

K. Marx
Manifesto of the Communist Party,
www.marxists.org/archive/marx/works/download/pdf/Manifesto.pdf

Capital. A Critique of Political Economy, Volume I

www.marxists.org/archive/marx/works/download/pdf/Capital-Volume-I.pdf

Critique of the Gotha Programme, www.marxists.org/archive/marx/works/1875/gotha/

L. Mises, Die Gemeinwirtschaft, Untersuchungen über den Sozialismus (Socialism: An Economic and Sociological Analysis), 2. Auflage, Fischer, Jena, 1932

A. Müller Lehning, Anarcho-Syndikalisme, Gem. Synd. Verb. 1927

O. Neurath, Wirtschaftsplan und Naturalrechnung (Economic Plan and Calculation in Kind), Berlin, 1925.

F. Pollock, Die planwirtschaftlichen Versuche in der Sowjetunion 1917-1927 (The Planned Economy Trials in the Soviet Union 1917–1927), Hirschfeld, 1929.

E. Varga, Die wirtschaftspolitischen Probleme der proletarischen Diktatur (The economic problems of the proletarian dictatorship), Carl Hoym.

La Révolution proletarienne, Juli 1931.

Most Marxists do not like Marx. At least, they do not like the economic principles of communist society that Marx derived from his critique of capitalism. But most Marxists do not criticize Marx in this respect either; they prefer to interpret him.

"Fundamental Principles of Communist Production and Distribution," the now legendary 1930 pamphlet of the Group of International Communists, was both a detailed exposition of the communist mode of production, which Marx and Engels had only sketched out, and a fundamental critique of the revisionism of the political parties that invoked Marx.

This book contains a selection of articles published by members of the Group of International Communists in various periodicals between 1925 and 1936, whose critique has lost none of its relevance to this day.

This book is a tribute to the collective work of the Group of International Communists of Holland. Given the experiences with state communism in Russia, their "Fundamental Principles of Communist Production and Distribution," published in 1930, was an attempt to elaborate the economic basis of a communist society as outlined by Karl Marx and Friedrich Engels. Although their explanations have lost none of their original topicality, their text has remained a product of its time in the way they address the literature of that period. This paper, therefore, attempts to reintroduce the core statements of the "Fundamental Principles of Communist Production and Distribution" into the current debate on alternatives to capitalism.

Despite the wonders of technology in the 21st century, global hunger, no access to clean water, bitter poverty, and miserable working conditions accompany the globalized market economy. Not only in the so-called developing countries but the successful industrial nations as well, the official poverty reports point up the growing discrepancy between what is presented as the wealth of the nation in the gross national product and calculated as per capita income and that what the majority of the population gets from this.

The question of the alternative to these achievements of the global market economy begins with arguments against the market. The classic of this critical analysis – »Capital« by Karl Marx – thus inevitably enjoys a renaissance. The guy got it right!

CRITIQUE OF CAPITALISM

AND THE QUESTION OF THE ALTERNATIVE

RED & BLACK BOOKS

Mistakes in the explanation of the cause of a disturbing effect usually continue in a wrong proposal for a solution. Those who explain poverty as the result of market failure look for alternatives to market regulation. Those who explain poverty as a necessary consequence of the market-based production relationship want to abolish the market. Any alternative to capitalism is therefore only as good as the underlying explanation of the capitalist mode of production to which it is supposed to be an alternative. Accordingly, the present book is not about imagining a better world, regardless of the reasons for the worldwide impoverishment and misery of large parts of the population, but about deriving from the explanation of capitalism the basic principles of an economy beyond capitalism. Critique and alternative are thus brought together. The question of feasibility is thereby resolved by itself.

Printed in Great Britain
by Amazon